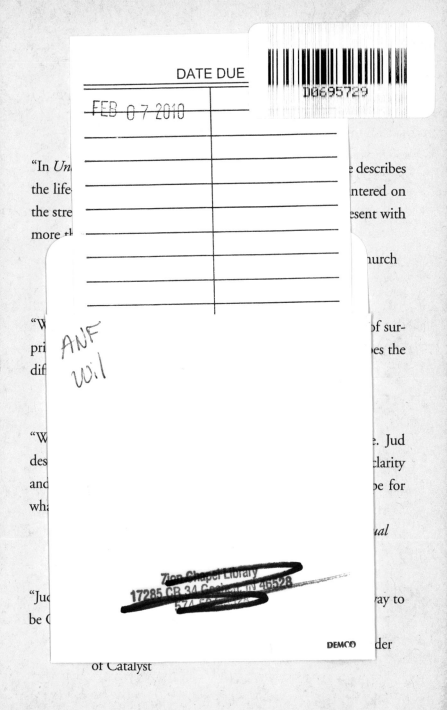

"In *Un* ... e describes
the life ... ntered on
the stre ... esent with
more th ...

... hurch

"W ... of sur-
pri ... es the
dif

"W ... e. Jud
des ... clarity
and ... be for
wha

ual

"Jud ... ay to
be C ...

... der
of Catalyst

"Reading *Uncensored Grace* will open your eyes to the wonders of God's saving love. It will give you hope that, no matter where you are in your 'process,' God is at work—and He is for you."

— CRAIG GROESCHEL, pastor of Lifechurch.tv, and author of *Chazown* and *Confessions of a Pastor*

"*Uncensored Grace* is filled with stories God must love!"

— JOHN ORTBERG, pastor at Menlo Park Presbyterian Church in California

"If you've given up dreams of ever finding a genuine fresh start in your life you ought to read this book. Real people. Real problems. Real hope. Get ready to be rocked by a fresh touch of amazing grace."

— GENE APPEL, lead pastor, Willow Creek Community Church, South Barrington, Illinois

"*Uncensored Grace* brings the brutal truth and the message of redemptive grace front and center. I was deeply moved and so inspired by these powerful and provocative stories of God's mercy. *Uncensored Grace* will transform your faith as you get a glimpse of how Jesus has set up shop on the streets of sin city."

— MIKE FOSTER, president of Ethur.org and founder of XXXchurch

EYES WIDE OPEN

SEE AND LIVE THE REAL YOU

JUD WILHITE
with Bill Taaffe

MULTNOMAH
BOOKS

EYES WIDE OPEN
PUBLISHED BY MULTNOMAH BOOKS
12265 Oracle Boulevard, Suite 200
Colorado Springs, Colorado 80921

ISBN 978-1-60142-072-5
ISBN 978-1-60142-243-9 (electronic)

Library of Congress Cataloging-in-Publication Data
Wilhite, Jud, 1971–
    Eyes wide open : see and live the real you / Jud Wilhite with Bill Taaffe. — 1st ed.
        p. cm.
    Includes bibliographical references.
    ISBN 978-1-60142-072-5 — ISBN 978-1-60142-243-9 (electronic)
  1. Identity (Psychology)—Religious aspects—Christianity. 2. Self-perception—Religious aspects—Christianity. 3. Christian life. I. Taaffe, William. II. Title.
    BV4509.5.W483 2009
    248.4—dc22

                                    2008050701

Printed in the United States of America
2009

10 9 8 7 6 5 4 3 2

SPECIAL SALES
Most WaterBrook Multnomah books are available at special quantity discounts when purchased in bulk by corporations, organizations, and special-interest groups. Custom imprinting or excerpting can also be done to fit special needs. For information, please e-mail SpecialMarkets@WaterBrookMultnomah.com or call 1-800-603-7051.

To John Ketchen and Keith Ray...
for helping me see

CONTENTS

Part 4: Wide Open to Influence

INTRODUCTION

I've always been freakish about my eyes. If anything or anyone gets close to them, I flinch, duck, or awkwardly step away. I can't wear contacts. I can't even put eye drops directly into my eyes. Instead, I have to put the drops on my eyelids and blink them in. Pretty pathetic, I know. If my friends want to gross me out, all they have to do is reach up and touch their eyes, and I'm done. Let's just say LASIK surgery isn't in my future.

One of the most traumatizing movies I've ever seen is *Minority Report,* in which people in the future are subjected to iris scans wherever they go. Tom Cruise's character even secretly gets his eyes replaced by a surgeon in order to avoid detection. I'll never forget sitting in the theater watching that scene, one eye closed and the other barely open, begging director Steven Spielberg to stop.

> We will explore what it means to live with eyes wide open, to embrace God's view instead of our own.

Metaphorically, this book is about getting a new set of eyes to see differently. Don't worry; there are no iris scans or black-market eye surgeons involved. But we will explore what it means to live with eyes wide open, to embrace God's view instead of our own.

Too many of us live with a distorted perspective of God. We see God as an all-powerful police officer aiming His speed gun at us. We believe that God loves; we just aren't convinced at the core of our being that He loves *us.* We think He's good, but we're acutely aware that *we* aren't. No matter how many messages we hear about grace, we wonder if we are forgiven. And we either jump on the performance treadmill to try and earn God's love, or we wallow in guilt and condemnation. Perhaps we run from the God thing altogether.

This distorted perspective also affects how we see ourselves. We look in the mirror, and instead of seeing one loved and forgiven by God, created in His image, empowered to influence the world for Him, we see something else. We see images from the past. Maybe it's the parent who was always critical of us, the schoolyard bully who picked on us, or the boss who laid us off still popping up in our memories. We play the destructive video clip over and over in our minds and come to the same conclusion: *I'm a failure...fat... insignificant...ugly...worthless...dumb...hopeless...unworthy... unloved...a nobody.*

If this sounds familiar to you, then I need to warn you about something: Distorted images are not only shaping your perspective but are also hindering your possibilities. If you see yourself as insignificant long enough, you'll start to act accordingly. If you see yourself as ugly or worthless, it will affect how you relate to your family and friends, your God, and your world. Rather than grow and change as you could, you'll be tempted to give in or give up or stay in a holding pattern of self-destructive behavior. Rather than make your own unique contribution in the world, you may pull back and settle for mediocrity. But this is not the real you.

Embracing God's perspective of you—living with eyes wide open—is so important because it allows you to become the person God created you to be. Not the you your critics claim you are. Not the you who pretends to be perfect in order to satisfy others' expectations. Not the you who feels guilty before God about your past and who lives with chronic spiritual remorse. Not the you who looks in the mirror and sees a failure.

The real you emerges as you see differently, *biblically.* You see yourself in light of who God says you are in His written Word. This is the first part of the adventure, but it doesn't end there. Then you begin to live out of this recognition. You are empowered to make the changes in your life that God desires you to make and to influence your world more fully for Him.

This is what *Eyes Wide Open* is all about. So welcome—this message is for you.

I've been on a journey of God-discovery and self-discovery for the past twenty years as a follower of Jesus. *Eyes Wide Open* began as I sat down with my journal and reflected on the most transforming principles that helped me move from being broken and hurting, with a distorted view of God and myself, to healing and growing as the real me.

> The real you emerges as you see yourself in light of who God says you are in His written Word.

As I've taught these principles to thousands of people, I've been humbled by the response. Some of the most "together" people I know have admitted to going through incredible struggles to accept God's grace, to see themselves with their new identity in Christ, and to make an impact in the world as a result of that. One of the greatest joys of my life has been to see them look at God and themselves with new eyes, freed to discover the person God designed them to be.

I'm excited to think about how this same message, conveyed through this book, can have the same transforming effect on *you*. An adventure of discovery and risk awaits you. I consider it a privilege to be your guide.

In the following pages, we'll look in much more depth at what it means to see and live with eyes wide open. For now, let me give you some glimpses of what you can expect.

- *Wide open to God.* Part 1 of this book looks at how God sees us and explores the awesome dimensions of His love and grace. We'll be challenged to move beyond clichés and feel-good spirituality and to internalize what it means to see God as a loving Father who is for us and has bound Himself to us by a spiritual agreement. Receiving His uncensored grace frees us to become the person He desires.

- *Wide open to identity.* Part 2 looks at the new identity the Bible declares we have. In the Christian community, we focus a lot on practical expressions of faith, such as prayer or service, but not enough on our position "in Christ" from which these practical expressions flow. So here we'll see how important our new identity is and discover that we are chosen and hidden in Christ. We'll learn the power of seeing ourselves as a priest, saint, and servant *now,* even if we don't always act as such.

- *Wide open to change.* Part 3 looks at how we come to express our new identity in everyday life. No matter where we're starting from, we can morph into the person God desires. This transformation does not mean we will come to look less like our own selves and more like everyone else. It means, instead, that we will more fully become the unique creation God made us to be.

- *Wide open to influence.* Part 4 looks at the importance of fulfilling the role in the world that God calls us to. We aren't fully ourselves until we are making the impact God desires for us to make. By embracing His view of us and living out of that, we can affect culture for the good and bring a little heaven to earth.

In the adventure you're about to undertake, you'll learn to see yourself as God created you—the real you, without pretense or playacting. This doesn't mean you'll have it all worked out by the end. You may still feel like a mess (just as I do at times). But now, as someone has put it, you'll be *God's mess.* And He has wonderful things in store for you.

Choose to see yourself from God's point of view. Sure, you're flawed, but you're also deeply loved. You're on a journey, and you're being changed into the person God created you to be.

Ready now? Open your eyes.

Part 1

———

Wide Open to God

Chapter 1

SEEING GOD CLEARLY

I once lost my glasses while running late for an appointment. I'm nearsighted, so I can see okay up close with or without my glasses. But if I get twenty or thirty feet away, forget it.

So here I was, looking all over the house, trying to find my glasses. I looked in the bedroom. I looked downstairs in the kitchen. I looked in my study. I was getting frustrated and angry, and then I went around the corner and saw my wife, Lori.

"You have to help me," I told her. "I'm running late and I can't find my glasses."

She looked at me with a puzzled stare and said, "Jud, they're on your face. You are *wearing* your glasses."

All I could say was "Uh…I am?" (I also had a fleeting thought that I'll be headed to a rubber room one day soon!)

> The amazing thing is that we are looking for what we already have, if only we had eyes to see it.

How foolish is that? I searched desperately for something right under, or rather *on,* my nose. But I'm not alone in this oddity.

We often look for what is right in front of us. We search for something to declare that our life has value. We look for someone to love us no matter how many indiscretions we've committed or what a mess we've made of our lives. We seek respect, validation, and significance. We run on a speeding approval treadmill, but it's never enough. And the amazing thing is that we are looking for what we already have, if only we had eyes to see it.

For years after I came to faith in Jesus Christ, I struggled to believe that God cared about me. I felt as if I had done so many bad things in my life that God could never fully accept me. No matter what I did, a small, quiet voice would come back and say, *Oh, you are just a mess, Jud. You're never going to amount to anything.*

I jumped through all the right religious hoops and went above and beyond to prove things to myself and others. Yet I'd still hear these thoughts: *Who are you kidding? Get real, man. You have too much stuff in your past.*

I was very aware of my abysmal failure to live up to God's standards on my own. I was worn out from trying to be good enough. I had buried the person God made me to be in order to fit the mold of what I perceived a Christian was.

All of it was part of my search for acceptance. But it wasn't working. I loved God, but it felt as if I was always performing for Him. I felt like a fake and sensed that God was as weary of the performance as I was.

I became so frustrated that I finally sat down and prayed, *God, I quit. If we're going to have any kind of relationship, it is up to You. I can't do this anymore.* And I was serious.

Maybe you can relate. Many people walk around feeling like spiritual failures.

Like the guy who said he loved Jesus but couldn't be a Christian. What is *that* about? After all, one would presume that the definition of a Christian is somebody who loves Jesus.

So this guy was asked, "How would you define a Christian?"

He said, "A Christian is someone who has his stuff together."

Really?

You know what I feel like sometimes? Like those fifteen-year-old pickup trucks you sometimes see rolling down the highway, loaded to the max with paint buckets and ladders and rakes and toolboxes and junk and a roll of unsecured carpet about to fall off and hit some innocent car right in the grille.

Christians have their stuff together—r-i-i-i-g-h-t.

I don't even try to pretend I have my stuff together anymore. But back when I was still thinking that I had to make myself worthy of God's love, my frustration continued to grow. Then one day I heard a talk from the Bible, where it says, "This is real love—not that we loved God, but that he loved us and sent his Son as a sacrifice to take away our sins."[1]

> I saw the key to living with my eyes wide open. I surrendered my view of myself and embraced God's view of me.

After the talk, I hurried out the door and went to a quiet place. The impact of this Bible passage floored me. For the first time, God's love began to sink in with all its implications. Somehow, in that act of giving up my personal quest for God's approval, I finally saw what had been there all along. And what I saw flipped my faith experience right-side up. It impacted every aspect of my relationships with others and changed my future. I saw the key to living with my eyes wide open. *I surrendered my view of myself and embraced God's view of me.*

I'd had it all backward. I was putting so much pressure on myself to earn God's love, but it was already there. While I had known this in my head, I had not accepted it in my heart.

The main thing is not my love for God but His love for me. And from that love I respond to God as one deeply flawed yet loved. I'm not looking to prove my worth. I'm not searching for acceptance. I'm responding from the worth God has already declared I have. And it isn't based on how I feel; it is based on His own promise and revelation in the Bible.

I don't have to act like someone else. Now I am free to become fully myself, the unique person God created me to be. My eyes opened wide.

How about you? Are you trying to perform so that God will love you? Are you working hard to keep all the plates spinning? Can you admit that it isn't working? Are you worn out and ready to quit?

I mean, do you believe deep down inside that God already loves you? Not your friend or your neighbor or the world in general, but *you*? Not your potential or your performance, not your achievements or your awards, not your title or your position, but *you,* right now, in the mess and mire of your life? Not in some trite sense, but in a deeply personal, real way?

Do you believe that God loves you when your prayers are weak? When your faith falters? When you lust after the guy or girl walking down the street? When you aren't sure of anything?

Do you believe that He loves you when you blatantly disregard His principles to serve a selfish desire? Do you believe, deep inside, that there is nothing you could do to cause Him to love you less?

I'm not surprised at people's reactions when I ask these questions. Most often people look down, avoid eye contact, and voice either an unconvinced yes or a blatant no. Many fall back on the right churchy answer about God's love—in theory at least. But when it comes to internalizing it, most seem to feel anything but loved.

> Living with eyes wide open means you don't have to be better looking, lose weight, wear different clothes, or achieve one more thing in your career. You matter just as you are.

Living with eyes wide open means you don't have to be better looking, lose weight, wear different clothes, or achieve one more thing in your career. You don't have to climb the ladder one more notch or accomplish another goal. You matter just as you are. You are an incredible spiritual being because that's how God created you.

Can you see it?

Chapter 2

COMING TO
OUR SENSES

A few years ago, the Wilhite family was flying across the country, all packed into our three-seat row. I was on the aisle. My wife, Lori, was in the window seat. Emma, who was almost four at the time, had the middle seat. And our little guy, Ethan, was in Lori's lap, except while I was reading, which was when he wanted to bother me by crawling onto my lap and pushing my book away.

I've come to the conclusion that flying is a horrible thing to inflict on parents. Parents just aren't equipped by God to deal with kids on airplanes. Before I had children, I'd look at kids who were out of control during flights and think, *Jeez, will you parents get a grip on your kids? You're letting them bother everyone!*

Now that's me.

So we were flying across the country. Ethan was one year old— a very powerful one-year-old if you know what I mean. His greatest delight in life at the time was pulling his sister's hair. Nothing gave him more excitement than to walk up, grab her hair with both hands, and yank.

She would scream bloody murder. He would get parents from both sides of the house running into the room to find out what was going on. Then he would just look at us and smile. It was all about *control,* you see.

Well, Ethan got into his superactive mode on the airplane, which we had learned was a sign that something big was about to happen. Lori turned to me with a look of half dread and half resignation in her eyes. And then it happened.

All of a sudden Ethan stood up in Lori's lap, grabbed the hair of the lady in the seat in front of him, and executed a full-tilt yank before Lori could stop him. The woman screeched, pulled herself away, and ducked down in the small space in front of her. She was freaking. We were mortified.

When everybody within three rows turned around to look at us with condemning frowns on their faces, I was tempted to say, "Whose kid is this? How did he get in *our* row?"

But it really doesn't matter what Ethan does because he's my son and I love him completely. Yes, there are moments when I'd like to wring his neck. But the truth is, God has put it into parents' DNA to love their children no matter how much they disappoint us. Unconditional parental love is a powerful force, and it explains a lot about the joy and frustration that are so much a part of parenthood.

We hope our kids will turn out all right. We pray for them. We sacrifice for them. Many of us would lay down our lives for them. So what happens when they're standing in district court on a drug possession charge? What gives when they've lost *another* job and want to move back home? Be honest. We still love them beneath the frustration.

Maybe two teenagers shared a moment of passion in the back-seat of a car. Now the girl is pregnant, and two families' lives are irreversibly changed. Do we still love them? They're our flesh and blood. Of course we do. And that's why the pain is as intense for us, if not more so, as it is for them.

I think this is why the picture of God as a loving Father is so prevalent in the Bible.

For a long time I didn't see God as loving. I saw God more as an angry being who shot lightning bolts and gave you zits on the day of your senior prom.

God was like my banker. Not that He was providing money but that He was always keeping score. Checking my credit limit. Looking over my shoulder.

"Jud, how are you doing?" I imagined God saying. "Uh-oh, during the Cowboys game, you yelled things at the TV that I can't repeat. A minus 2 there. Hey, you didn't respond well in traffic. A minus 5. Well, I did see how you helped that homeless guy. So a plus 5 there. Remember when you were ready to be sarcastic in front of the checkout clerk but held yourself back and smiled? I'll give you a plus 3."

I was always trying to do enough to stay plus 1, to stay out of the red zone.

My view of God impacted my relationship with Him. And how I saw Him affected how I saw everything else. This is why having a correct view of God is so important. Without it, we wallow in guilt or are paralyzed by fear. We continually view God as a banker or Santa Claus or the Big Guy in the Sky, but we miss seeing God first as a loving Father.

One of my favorite stories that Jesus told is a well-known tale about two brothers and their father.[1] Neither of the sons in the story has a very loving view of his father, whose role in the story provides a picture of God.

The younger son goes to his dad, who is obviously well-off, and asks for his share of the family estate, pronto. The people who heard Jesus tell this story would have been shocked by the son's audacity—not because he wanted his share but because it was a huge insult to go to his father in such a gimme-gimme way before the father had even passed away. In essence the son is saying, "Dad, drop dead. I want my loot."[2]

As you might imagine, the younger son gets his inheritance, sells off his share, and parties his brains out. He basically goes to Vegas and lives *la vida loca*!

Finally, at the end, he's broke. He has no more friends. He has bottomed out, sleeping in the gutter, longing to eat the pods that the pigs ate—which, for a Jew especially, had to be the ultimate degradation. Then "he came to his senses."[3]

I love that phrase. It implies that he was not only far from home but also far from his real self. He literally came to himself.

This describes a lot of my own journey. In junior high, I began my experiment with drugs, and it dominated my life through my high school years. My drug use was a dark secret that I kept tucked away as much as I could. During that season of my life I was an expert deceiver and spent way too much time serving my own addiction and desires at the expense of everyone else.

I eventually become so tired of the mess I had made that I came to my senses. I reluctantly decided to return to God, half-afraid He'd zap me for all the things I had done. But God forgave me and accepted me when I had nothing to offer Him but brokenness.

To this day I haven't gotten over that. I see it as a great irony that He'd take someone like me and use me to help others find their way home. But God is a God of surprises just like that.

We see this bent toward surprises when the younger son in Jesus' story comes to his senses and returns home. He realizes he has to go back to his father. He has to make things right. He has to ask his dad to forgive him. He has to start over, and the only place where he has any hope of getting help is at home.

Think of this kid—it has to be brutal for him. He thinks about the debt he owes his father. He remembers all the pain he has caused his family. He goes back with a rehearsed speech about how he would settle for being just one of his father's working hands. He's not worth anything more.

Yet when he gets near home, his father is thrilled. He who was gone—forever, as far as his dad knew—has returned. The father sees him coming from a long way off, then runs toward him, throws his arms around his son, and kisses him.

There's no bitterness from the father about the son squandering his fortune. No payback plan to recover the lost riches. No house arrest for the next year until the son "proves" himself.

You'd think the father might send him to the quarry to hammer stones for the next decade. Make him earn his keep by sweeping out the chicken coops for five straight years. *Yeah, that'll show this little brat. That'll teach him.* In fact, there is a similar story in Buddhist literature, and in it the father does make the son spend his life working off all the wrong he has done.

This is where the picture of God in the Bible is so radically different. There is just amazing love and forgiveness. The father *runs* to greet his son. He's not holding back, trying to settle the score. No calculating. No payback. He doesn't talk about the sins of the past.

> The picture of God in the Bible is so radically different. There is just amazing love and forgiveness.

He's not double-checking his son's credit report from the last three years. He's not acting like an accountant.

The father gets a robe and puts it on his son. He orders that a fattened calf be killed in his son's honor. In other words, he's saying, "We're going to have a feast."

It's party time! They strike up the music.

This is how God accepts people when they return to Him.

A few years ago, a member of our faith community posted this message to God online:

God, I miss You. I know it wasn't You who left, or stopped
coming, or took a step away. I hope that You would come back
to me with the strength and vigor of my younger days.... Now
I'm bogged down with relationships, bills, family issues, job
worries, school issues, and amidst all of this, I have lost sight,
lost the scent, grown deaf to the sounds, dull to the taste, and
numb to the feeling of Your very presence. And I feel so very
alone.... God, I miss You. I'll try to come home soon.[4]

Have you ever felt like the woman who wrote those words? Ever
felt like your spiritual passion has dried up? Like life's bogged you
down and your soul has grown numb? Like you're just going
through the motions? Like you're spiritually far from home?

When I read that post, I wanted to reach through the computer
and tell the writer that God desires nothing more than for her to
come home. That He is a Father who loves her passionately.

Jesus called God "Abba," which is an Aramaic term of endear-
ment for *father*.[5] The closest we can get to it in English is probably
daddy. If we only understood how shocking this use of the word was
in its day!

Calling God "Abba" was revolutionary. No one in the history of
Jewish religious teaching, no one in the history of other religions,
had ever said you could basically call God "Daddy."[6]

You may read the words *daddy* or *father* and be unable to square
them up with your own dad. Yet the model of a father is the model
set forth in the Scriptures. The paradigm is God Himself.

Jesus taught that God is holy and that God is also Daddy. It's mind-boggling if you think about it. It means that we can run into His arms as a child would because He's a loving Father who cares—really *cares*—about what's going on in our lives.

When you start relating to God as a loving Father, not just paying lip service to this relationship but really *relating* to Him, then you realize that God's heart is for all His children. For His children who are secure, yes. But just as importantly for His children who are wayward, broken, hurting, and maybe living wild lives far from home. All of us know how to find the mud pretty fast. All of us have made messes in our lives.

In this society there's so much static and twenty-four-hour news and entertainment cycles and ad campaigns and scams and lust for money and sex that every urge or desire seems to be an imperative. Yet the real imperative in life is to come to our senses and relate to God as Abba.

Take some time to reflect upon the power of this image. See it clearly. The Father is running with His arms open wide toward *you*.

Chapter 3

UNCENSORED GRACE

Living with eyes wide open means seeing God as more than just a Father running toward us. He is also a Judge, taking upon Himself the punishment we deserve and offering uncensored, undomesticated grace.

When I reflect on grace, I think of Duane "Dog" Chapman, star of the A&E reality TV show *Dog the Bounty Hunter*. He tracks down fugitives, brings them in despite risk to life and limb, tells them they need to get right with God, and offers them a cigarette. At the core, Dog is trying to find his way and live out his life—bad language, nicotine, and all.

Some of us at our church felt that Dog would be a perfect fit for the role of guest speaker. After all, as a bounty hunter, he claims to be in the second-chance business, just as we are in the church. So we extended him an invitation, and he agreed to come and share his story.

I interviewed Dog during eight weekend services—five live and three more by video. As we found out, Dog grew up in a tough neighborhood of Denver. Later he was arrested *eighteen times* for armed robbery. He ended up spending time in prison for murder one, not as the triggerman but for being present at a fatal drug-related shooting. In the Texas legal system at the time, that made Dog as guilty as the guy who fired the weapon.

That event marked a turning point for Dog. "As I was entering prison," he said, "I made up my mind that I was going to change back into something my mother had planned. I changed my life at that second, even though I did eighteen months behind bars after that."

Dog owed two hundred dollars a month in child support when he got out of prison. He couldn't find a job because of his criminal record. Dog's judge, however, heard that Dog had run down an escaping inmate while in prison. So when Dog got out, the judge said to him, "I have this guy who ran away. He's wanted for sexually assaulting a child. Can you go and get him? I'll pay you if you do."

Dog, who is as street-smart a guy as there is, was happy to oblige. "Sure," he said. "I'll go get the guy."

Thinking like a criminal would, Dog nabbed the guy quickly. Soon the judge tossed him the names of six other men to capture. Eventually he referred Dog to a bail bondsman, and the rest is TV history. Dog has now been a bounty hunter for thirty years. He's caught more than six thousand people.

Over the years, Dog came to realize the fleeting nature of life. He put his trust in Jesus and turned his life over to Him.

At one point, when their show was first beginning, he and his wife, Beth, faced a crossroad. A major network was offering them a lot more money to do the show than A&E was, but with one stipu-

lation: they couldn't use the name of Jesus on the air or pray to God.
A&E offered less but didn't care if they prayed to Methuselah, as
long as they brought in fugitives and treated people well.

Dog and Beth were genuinely tempted to go with the larger network. Then one day they pulled their car over in their home state of
Hawaii and looked at each other. They both knew at that moment
that they had to go with the smaller network. In their words, "We
had to go with God." So they took the risk and jumped on board.

Dog sat with me on the stage at Central Christian Church and
offered people the opportunity to turn their lives over to God and
experience the same grace he has known. Hundreds of people
responded. What I'll never forget is that after the first two services
on Saturday, as we were standing in a backstage hallway, Dog had
huge tears in his eyes.

"Jud," he said, "thirty years ago someone said to me that one day
I'd be used to help people come to God. Yours is the first church to
allow me that privilege, and I thank you for it."

And then Dog swallowed me up in a hug.

It was a moment for both of us. We had just seen all these people cross the line of faith in their lives. We both stood there in tears
at the amazing grace of God in using two imperfect people like us to
help others.

Throughout that weekend, tens of thousands of people came to hear
Dog's story, and many lives were touched for good. Dog and Beth
were on a spiritual high afterward, as were we.

And then, about six months after that weekend, Dog made the phone call. You remember the one I'm talking about, don't you? The secretly recorded call to his son in which he made those horrible racial slurs? The call in which he used the n-word six times in relation to his son's girlfriend, with whom he had strong differences? The story was news fodder throughout the world. In a matter of seconds, Dog went from being a beloved rock-star bounty hunter to someone who was anathema. His show was removed from the air for four months, not returning until the spring of 2008.

I certainly won't defend what Dog said. It was awful and wrong, by his own admission. Hearing Dog's side of the story in detail at least gives some context and a better understanding. But you're still left with those words in all their shamefulness.

I found the entire situation somewhat bizarre, especially considering that Dog's pastor, Tim Storey, is African American. They've been close friends for years and talk monthly on the phone.

But all of that aside, what do you do when someone has really blown it? How do you respond?

Did that phone call negate the positive effect Dog has had on many people's lives? Did it undo the spiritual decisions many took in our own church, including those by people of color? Did it forever alter Dog Chapman's position with God?

No.

It simply proved that Dog needs what we all need—grace. Not just any kind of grace, not domesticated grace, but what I call uncensored grace. Here's how I described it in a previous book, *Uncensored*

Grace: Stories of Hope from the Streets of Vegas:

> Uncensored grace is what you get from loving God when all
> the religious types have gone home, and every last hope for
> your own effort has blown up in your face. Uncensored
> means that there is no formula or membership or perfor-
> mance that stands between you and God's goodness. Uncen-
> sored means that as wide and deep and high as your
> mountain of personal ruin might get, God's transforming
> grace is always wider and deeper and higher.[1]

Dog has found that grace and is trying to move forward and make things right with those he has hurt. He's continuing in the second-chance business.

Uncensored grace is not simply grace for when we first come to faith; it is grace for each day after, as we fail and struggle. It is one thing to come to God for salvation, but it is something else to experience His work of transformation over an extended period of time. One should lead to the other, and daily uncensored grace is what we all need desperately from our loving Father.

> Uncensored grace is not simply grace for when we first come to faith; it is grace for each day after, as we fail and struggle.

The Bible is a story of grace from beginning to end. Some of the greatest characters in its pages needed a radical form of grace. Take David, the king of Israel. We've made him the subject of paintings, sculptures, and poetry for thousands of years. He's a legend in the Bible, "a man after [God's] own heart."[2] Yet David did some unspeakable things.

One day David was walking on the roof of his palace when he noticed a woman bathing.[3] He had never seen her before, and his blood began to run at the sight of her. David immediately sent for her, found out her name was Bathsheba, and learned that she was married to a guy named Uriah, who happened to be out of town fighting in a war for David.

David slept with her, and she became pregnant. As if this betrayal wasn't bad enough, David then tried to cover his tracks. He thought he could make things okay if he could get Uriah home quickly to sleep with Bathsheba. That way Uriah would think he was the baby's father. Believe me, *Desperate Housewives* has nothing on the Bible.

Uriah came back from the battlefield at David's request. David asked him for an update on the battle and then told Uriah to go home and spend the night with his wife before he went back to the battlefield. Uriah left David, but he didn't go home. He slept outside the palace doors because he didn't feel right about sleeping with his wife while his men were fighting.

David hadn't just punk'd somebody's husband. He had messed with a really good dude. So the next night David had Uriah to dinner, got him drunk, and told him to go home and see his wife. But Uriah refused and slept outside again.

Think about this insanity. Here was God's king, committing adultery, lying, deceiving, even trying to get a guy loaded to implement his twisted will. Man, was this ever messed up!

David now took his most drastic measure. He sent word to the leader of the army to have Uriah placed on the front lines. David knew that if Uriah was placed there, he was almost certain to be killed in battle. This plan worked and Uriah died. Add cold-blooded murder to the list.

What David needed was not some trite kind of forgiveness. He didn't simply need someone to tell him it was all good because he felt bad about it. If this were to happen in our day, David would be slaughtered by the press, would be sued for millions, and would likely spend time in prison. And that doesn't include the cover story the *National Enquirer* would do on him.

What David needed was uncensored grace.

We see David's desire for uncensored grace in Psalm 51. He cried out to God for forgiveness, saying, "I recognize my rebellion; it haunts me day and night."[4]

Have you ever had something haunt you day and night? Something that follows you, gets into your dreams at night, and tweaks your perceptions of reality? Something from your past maybe? Something you would never tell anyone else? Something you wish with all your might you could just make go away?

Maybe, as with David, it involved sexual sin and deception. Or maybe you kept the secret of a gambling problem from your loved ones, and they've never known about the money you've wasted that was equally theirs.

Maybe you cheated on a boyfriend or girlfriend. *Oh, it was just a one-night stand. No one will ever know.* Maybe you have intentionally exaggerated the truth to impress school friends or work associates. *Jeez, how could that ever be wrong?* Perhaps you've been hiding an addiction. *Look, I can't tell anybody. It's probably better that they don't know.*

For years I've been haunted by decisions I made while caught up in my addiction to drugs. I have prayed with David, "Against you, and you alone, have I sinned; I have done what is evil in your sight."[5]

> When you and I make Jesus our leader and forgiver, we're offered forgiveness because of who God is and what He has done for us. It's called grace. And it's uncensored.

The thing about God is He doesn't respond with something trite like "No problem. Forget about it." The Bible says that God is just and that there must be a penalty for sin. But rather than punish us, He sent His Son, Jesus, who took upon Himself the sins of the world. He bore the punishment that I, Jud Wilhite, deserved. You can join me if you'd like and substitute your own name here. When you and I make Jesus our leader and forgiver, we're offered forgiveness because of who God is and what He has done for us. It's called grace. And it's uncensored.

This has been hard for me to accept. For years I'd wake up in the morning and ask God to forgive me for my past addiction and the pain I caused the people I loved most. I would do extra religious duty, so to speak, hoping to win points with God and erase my past.

Many of us do this, and it often forms a high obstacle to God.

I talked to one man at church who told me that every single day for the past ten years he had asked God to forgive him for the same thing. Every day for ten years!

He said, "Jud, what do I do?"

I told him to go to Psalm 51, read it, and offer it up as a personal prayer, asking God again to forgive and cleanse him.

"Then—and this is important—," I said to him, "after asking forgiveness, don't ever ask God to forgive you for that sin again."

He actually took a step back when I said that. I had freaked him out. So I repeated myself: "As your pastor, I'm telling you: Ask forgiveness once more, and don't ever ask God to forgive you for that sin again. He has already forgiven you. He has let it go, but you keep bringing it up every morning."

I shared with him that the Bible says, "He has removed our sins as far from us as the east is from the west."[6] The cool thing is that you can go to absolute north and south, but there is no absolute east and west. He has removed our sins from us as far as is possible. This man needed to accept God's grace. He needed to stop bringing up his sin and start living as one forgiven!

> After I've asked God for forgiveness, I believe He gives it, and I move forward. I don't keep bringing up the things He has already forgiven me for.

That's what I've done in my life, and it has made a real difference. I still ask for forgiveness when I fail—that is a biblical thing to do. But after I've asked God for it, I believe that He gives it, and I move forward. I take Him at His word that He has removed my sins from me and that He can still use me. I don't keep bringing up the things He has already forgiven me for.

Last year, a good friend sent me an e-mail saying that he had thought of me when he read this passage from Psalm 51: "I will teach your ways to rebels, and they will return to you."[7] He thanked me for teaching God's ways to rebels like him.

I sat at my computer and cried.

I know I'm a softie, but I'm so thankful that I experienced uncensored grace and that I can share it with others. My tears were tears of joy at God's goodness.

David was saying in Psalm 51 that if God forgave him and restored him, David would leverage that to impact others—and he did. There were still consequences to be paid for his actions—painful consequences. But because David accepted uncensored grace and lived in it, God used him to accomplish many important things after this. David, a forgiven adulterer and murderer, ultimately defeated his enemies, kept the country unified, and named his son Solomon as his successor.

Have you opened your heart wide to God's uncensored grace?

Chapter 4

QUESTIONS THAT CHANGED MY LIFE

Many people believe in God, but they still don't really believe that God is *for* them. They often think God is getting even with them for things they've done.

Like Tim. Six years ago, when he was a married man, he had an affair with a woman married to someone else. A lot of pain and heartache came from the drama when Tim's secret became known. But since then he has taken steps to make things right with his ex, with his kids, and with God. Yet when his most recent job deteriorated, he wondered if God wasn't pulling a fast one on him to get back at him.

And like Sarah. She was an adult dancer in her early twenties. Now she's in her late twenties and has left that lifestyle behind. She has tried hard but just hasn't found the right guy to spend the rest of her life with. You know what she thinks deep down? That God might be making her suffer for the things she did in the strip clubs.

God is into forgiveness, not payback.

This is absurd. God is into forgiveness, not payback. This is exactly what the Bible gets at when it asks, "If God is for us, who can be against us?"[1]

One afternoon, this passage really sunk in for me as I lay on my hammock in the backyard.

Since living in the Las Vegas area, I've felt that the sky provides an awareness of God and a touch of reality. At ground level the city never sleeps. The roulette wheels forever spin. Inside the casinos there is a surreal sense of timelessness. But walk outside and look up. The sky is vast, enveloping the earth. It's the antidote to the mire below.

I turned the question over in my mind while looking at the clouds drifting by that day. *If God is for us, who can be against us?* In the first part of the question, the "if" isn't really casting any doubt. It is in fact assuming the truth of what it states. God is for us! He's *for* us. Looking at it another way, He's for *us*!

The God who created the sky, the trees, the landscape, the clouds—*that* God. The God who created the universe—*that* God. The God who is spinning our planet on its axis right now at a thousand miles an hour, ensuring that we travel 1.3 million miles today in our orbit around the sun—*that* God. The God who has the expanse of the universe in the palm of His hand. The God who created the complexities of the human eye, the human cell, and the DNA strand. That God is for us—for *us*!

And if He is for us, then "who can be against us?"

At first glance, a lot of people can be against us. It may be our teacher or our employer or that guy who put a knife in our back last year. The IRS may seem to be out to get us. At times our family members may feel more like enemies than friends. Sometimes I've felt like I was against *myself*!

But this question does not imply that if God is for us we'll have no more problems. It's saying that if God is for us, no matter what difficulty, pain, or hardship we face, God will pull us through. He will fight for us in the midst of the problem.

God is not holding our mistakes over us and trying to punish us. He loves to forgive and empower.

Now, this doesn't mean there aren't consequences for our actions. There is definitely a biblical principle that what people sow they eventually reap,[2] and sometimes the consequences are a bear to live with.

But there are also consequences and results for how we see God. We reap what we sow there too. If we see God as some kind of celestial book-keeper always about to strike us down, we'll definitely pay a price. One consequence is that we'll probably live in an awful cycle of fear, frustration, and guilt. Seeing with eyes wide open means seeing that God is for us.

> No matter what difficulty, pain, or hardship we face, God will pull us through. He will fight for us in the midst of the problem.

Tina is frustrated because her life just doesn't seem to be working. She has been clean and sober for five years, but she is dealing with a constant anger problem. The smallest thing sets her off, and she finds herself regularly screaming at her husband and two stepsons.

Recently she hasn't even wanted to get out of bed in the morning. She's also down on herself for rarely visiting her mom during the six months she was in a hospital. When Tina's mom died, she died alone.

Afterward Tina found her mom's journal, going back decades. "My daughter is driving me crazy," her mom wrote when Tina was a kindergartner. "How can a five-year-old be so loving one minute and so hateful the next?"

Tina said that most of her adult life she has wondered about that haunting question. Why is she so angry with others? Now she thinks it's just her pathetic nature. In her mind it's as if God doesn't need someone awful like her around.

She believes that if she could just live according to God's Word, she would have a happy and abundant life. But she doesn't have that kind of life, so it all comes back on her. If she weren't such a loser, she could do life right. She's constantly crying out to God to help her break the cycle.

One of the first things I'd ask Tina is this: "What would happen if you stopped trying so hard? What if you gave yourself permission to reframe your thinking process about God, your parents, and yourself? What would happen if you internalized the idea that God is *for* you?"

Then I'd challenge her to begin and end the next several days by reflecting on the question "If God is for me, who can be against me?"

That question could change her life. It has changed mine. Something about the hammock and a perfect day and the massive bright blue sky drives it home when I need to experience it anew. *God's favor is real.* It's not just the power of positive thinking. This is the message of the Bible. Accepting this message deep in our souls is how renewal springs forth. Not more effort to be perfect but more awareness of our perfect God, who is for us.

So how can we be sure that God is really for us?

The answer comes in the form of another question in the next verse. "He who did not spare his own Son, but gave him up for us all—how will he not also, along with him, graciously give us all things?"[3]

God was willing to go to such crazy lengths so we could be in a right relationship with Him. He was willing to allow His Son to be beaten, tortured, mocked, spat upon, and crucified. If He would go to all that trouble because He loves you and me, will He not also meet our basic needs? Will He not help us with the details of our lives? Do we need any more proof that God is for us than the cross?

> Take that awful thing you did ten years ago or ten minutes ago, and think about it. If God would send Jesus and literally have Him die, how could He not forgive your sin no matter how horrible it is?

Take your secret sin—your most shameful habit, whatever it may be. Take that awful thing you did ten years ago or ten minutes ago, and think about it. If God would send Jesus and literally have Him die, how could He not forgive your sin no matter how horrible it is? How could He not be "for you"?

In fact, the Bible says that nothing can separate you from God's love in Christ. Not "death nor life, neither angels nor demons, neither the present nor the future, nor any powers, neither height nor depth, nor anything else in all creation."[4] Try that statement on for size— it's exhaustive. It covers all dimensions of time, space, and spirit.

The two questions in Romans 8 have made more of an impact on my life over the last decade than any others I've asked or been asked. They've changed how I see myself and my circumstances. They've given me hope when it felt like everything was falling apart. They've helped me live with eyes wide open.

Take some time to reflect on them and personalize them. Think about them on the drive to work. Post them over your bathroom mirror. Let them own you as much as you own them.

Question 1: If God is for you, who can be against you?

Question 2: He who did not spare his own Son, but gave him up for you—how will he not also, along with him, graciously give you all things?

Chapter 5

IF GOD IS FOR ME,
WHY IS LIFE SO HARD?

Okay, so all this talk about seeing my life from God's perspective is fine. But why is it that when I look around, I see so much pain? If God is Abba, if His grace is so available, if He is for me, then why is my life so hard?

We know these questions intimately. Sometimes life feels like the game Boggle. Remember Boggle? There are sixteen dice, each with a different letter on each of its multiple sides. Somebody shakes the dice and then lets them settle in their slots in the box. Then the players have three minutes to find as many words as possible from the random faceup letters.

The three minutes is the catch. You've never realized how much pressure a three-minute limitation can exert. There's a point system, of course. (Isn't that the way we think about life?) And naturally, whoever gets the most points wins.

Sometimes you look down at the dice, and the words seem to appear before your eyes. It makes sense immediately.

Other times you look and look—nothing. You feel like a failure. Just as your three minutes are up, the competitive jerk next to you (somebody is always competitive) says, "Look, dummy! The word *the* is right there!"

This is why I don't like games.

Still, I've decided that Boggle is a metaphor for life.

Aren't there times when you get all shaken up, just like those dice? Life throws stuff at you, and too often it seems as if there are three or four huge negatives for every positive.

It could be a spouse who sits down with you, calls you by your first name (which is ominous in itself because it doesn't normally happen), and lets you know the relationship is over. It could be a meeting with an employer who reams you out for something you never did. There's no use arguing because he wouldn't believe you in the first place. This sort of unfairness is the subtext of life on earth, isn't it?

Unexplained suffering boggles our mind, and if we're honest, our faith develops a hiccup.

Our world gets all shaken up like Boggle. Occasionally time gives us perspective, and we can make some sense out of it. But just as often, no matter how many angles we analyze it from, the situation makes no more sense years later than it did at the time it happened. It's a mystery, and no matter how much we pray, God doesn't explain it to us.

You've been there no doubt. Or if you haven't, you will be. God keeps His thoughts to Himself. We search and think and ask, *God, what are You up to?* All of it boggles our mind, and if we're honest, our faith develops a hiccup.

A few years ago I got to meet a single twenty-one-year-old woman who was so afraid of having a child that she hid her pregnancy from everyone she knew. She had no family nearby, so she told no one.

When the time came, she gave birth by herself in a dingy restroom at work. She had lived in denial the entire pregnancy. She was too terrified even to have a plan for what would happen at the end of nine months.

Once the child was born, the mother didn't know what to do, and this poor woman, totally alone, with no one to talk to, snapped. She disposed of the baby in a garbage can behind her workplace. There, in among the banana peels, cans, and hot-dog wrappers, the baby died.

Later that day, the owners of the business where the young woman worked became suspicious. And after some questions and a series of events, they found the baby's lifeless body in the trash, hours away from being hauled to the county dump.

Hearing the story on the news, I felt compelled to visit this young mother in jail. The person I met was a scared girl who had done a horrible thing out of desperation, confusion, and fear. The whole episode—the deed she had done, where she had come to, the pain and the horror that were still in her mind—just wrecked me for the baby and for the mother.

Several people in the community, including the young woman herself, concluded that the baby needed a proper funeral. They didn't know anyone who would do it, so I agreed to perform the ceremony.

I'll never forget the scene. Just a handful of people attended the service—down-to-earth people, working people. The baby's tiny casket was surrounded by flowers.

When the mother arrived, she was wearing an orange jail jump-suit. A chain had been wrapped around her waist and connected to her wrists. Other chains bound her ankles so that when she approached the grave site, she moved in tiny steps, a few inches at a time. No one was allowed to be near her, so she hobbled over to one side to watch.

After a few words and a prayer, we sang "Jesus Loves the Little Children." I looked over, and there was this young mother, weeping, in chains, looking at her child's casket. Everything in her wanted to rewind the clock a few days.

It was a tragic scene, awful in its finality, filled with questions about what kind of life the mother would now lead. Rarely has my heart been as heavy as it was that day. As I looked at her, I couldn't escape the thought, *Why is this world such a total mess?* To this day, the image of her, in prison jumpsuit and chains, standing by that lit-tle casket stirs emotion in me.

Where is she now? What became of her? I don't know, but God does.

Sometimes it's hard to accept that God is for us when so much evidence suggests the contrary. I mean, come on, just look at today's headlines. Someone has been shot at a convenience store (what a convenience—walk inside and *bang!*). Another carjacking has taken place (unfortunately this is so common that it's mentioned only because the car was parked at a police station). A tractor-trailer driver high on drugs comes over a rise at 11:00 p.m. and doesn't see the traffic jam in front of him. Cars are idling in the middle of the highway unable to move or get out of the way. The truckdriver plows into a sitting car, shears off its top, and kills three of the four people inside.

Where is God in this mess?

Now, I'm the first to confess that God isn't to blame for much of the stuff we see. God didn't invent guns used to kill school kids, or incest, or atomic weapons, or terrorism, or high-interest payday loan centers, or divorces that are as easy as buying potato chips. *We* did that. We human beings cause a lot of the heartache and pain we see in the world.

The Bible also speaks of a spiritual force of evil that wreaks havoc in our lives. This can explain much of the pain in our world, but there are still things that, if I'm honest with you, I just don't understand. Take the tsunami that hit the southeast Asian coast a few years ago. We try to figure it out, playing the cosmic mind game in our head, and all we're left with is "Okay, God, how does this fit together?"

Paul wrote to the believers in Rome and didn't gloss over the fact that we live in a world filled with pain. He described the situation in our world with terms like *suffering, frustration, bondage, decay,* and *dying.* Right in the middle of all this, Paul wrote, "We know that in all things God works for the good of those who love him, who have been called according to his purpose."[1]

In all *what*? How are we to understand "in all things"? Well, you name it. In suffering with chronic pain from the car accident you had as a teenager, in frustration with a difficult spouse in a bad marriage, in the decay of our planet due to neglect and abuse, in disappointment with being on Prozac, and on and on. In all this mess, God will actually take it and work it for good.

The Bible doesn't say we will immediately see results. It simply says that in *everything,* God works for the good of those who love Him and have been called by Him.

This sounds remarkable, doesn't it? And it is.

But these verses don't say that it's *all* good. We're still living in a world damaged by sin. Clearly some things that happen in our world are not good. They're hideous, hellacious.

Greg Boyd exchanged a series of letters with his unbelieving father, Ed Boyd, that were collected in a book entitled *Letters from a Skeptic.* In these letters, the question of suffering comes up several times. One of the most powerful is when Ed writes about his wife, Arlyle. He mentions that when she was dying, they all prayed and prayed, but it seemed like God didn't care.

Greg responded to his dad's letter straight from the gut. He recalled a time of struggling with his faith in college. One day, as he reflected on the horror of Auschwitz, he looked up at the sky and said in a loud, angry voice, "The only God I can believe in is one who knows firsthand what it's like to be a Jewish child buried alive and knows what it's like to be a Jewish mother watching her child be buried!"[2]

Greg says that's when it hit him. This is precisely what Christianity declares—that God comes right into the hell we make.

> I guess what I'm saying, Dad, is this. I don't know exactly why God didn't answer our prayers for Arlyle. I know that if it

wasn't for human sin, and if we weren't involved in this spiritual war, this painful situation never would have arisen. But more important than this explanation is this understanding: God was suffering with you, and me, and Arlyle, throughout the whole affair. He cries too. And through his participation in our pain, he wants to redeem it. He wants to bring about whatever healing is possible to you, and to me, and to all involved.[3]

What helped Greg deal with the loss of his mom was not primarily a logical answer. What helped was the person of Jesus, in whom he placed his faith.

I've talked to people who are struggling with the loss of a loved one or a life-altering tragedy. Some have said, "Jud, I don't have the emotional strength right now to believe."

I look them in the eye and say, "Okay, as your friend, I'm going to ask you to do something for me. I want you to let me believe for you. Let me carry your junk for the next few weeks. You just worry about putting one foot in front of the other, and don't give up. I'll pray for you even if you can't pray. I'll believe for you that God will bring you out of this darkness even if you can't believe."

> The Bible says that God isn't finished with us. The story isn't done.

See, the Bible says that God isn't finished with us. The story isn't done. It's a mistake to reach our conclusions based just on what we see around us right now. The most radical act we can take when we are beaten down by life is to stop and meditate on the fact that God is not finished.

He's not finished no matter how painful it is, no matter how hard some situation is to navigate through. The concluding chapter has yet to be written.

At times I feel worn out and used up, but God isn't finished.

Other times I feel confused and frustrated, but God isn't finished.

Sometimes I say things in anger and wallow in regret, but God isn't finished.

He's not done with me. He's not done with you. He's not done with the story of the world and the story of creation. A conclusion is coming. It's the promise of heaven that is held out from the earliest pages of the Bible. It's the paradise that *will* be regained by those who believe.

> There's a lot that I don't understand, but I know that God is good, and I accept that He is working for my good.

There's a lot that I don't understand, but I know that God is good, and I accept that He is working for my good. I believe it even though the plumber just left my house after informing me that the water damage above my kitchen means I need to have my entire shower torn out and retiled. Seriously, I have a hole in the ceiling of my kitchen that emits a funky smell. Then my wife's phone stopped syncing to her computer calendar, and our bulldog, Roxy, started peeing all over the furniture for no apparent reason—all this within ten minutes as I was writing this chapter. "Um, God, do You not like my writing?"

It takes *will* to believe that He is working for my good. The belief doesn't just float into my head. I need to consciously reflect on God and His promises. As I take Him at His word and rest in that,

I find that I'm still smiling—even though I've just lost a chunk of cash.

For most people, the spiritual life is accompanied by a sense of mystery. You never have all the answers and all the conclusions lined up. If you did, you'd be God. But when you accept that God is working in the mess of life, the pressure begins to lift. You have Jesus Christ to walk beside you even if the buildings are falling all around.

The Bible tells a story about a day when Jesus' disciples were out on the sea.[4] A fierce storm arose. The winds howled and the waves crashed, filling the small fishing boat with water.

Terrified, the disciples were struggling to keep their boat afloat when they apparently realized that Jesus was asleep in the stern. Here they were bailing like crazy to keep from going under, and He was sleeping!

The Bible puts it tactfully, but these guys were fishermen, and I suspect they knew how to speak like fishermen. Waking Him up, they asked, "Lord, do You not care if we die?" In other words, "What's the matter with You? Don't You give a rip that we're suffering and our lives are at stake?"

Fortunately the story doesn't end with the disciples' fear, anger, and sarcasm.

Jesus walked to the front of the boat and looked out at the crashing waves. He stared right into the storm and rebuked it, saying, "Silence! Be still!"[5]

Suddenly the wind stopped and the sea was so still that it looked like glass. Jesus turned to His disciples and, in one of the most understated lines in the Bible, said, "Why are you afraid? Do you still have no faith?"[6]

How about the storms in your life? Is your boat ready to capsize? Are you far from shore and ready to drown? Are you disoriented? Is time running out for you in the dead of night?

There is much we don't understand about why we suffer. But the fact is, we do suffer.

One person, just one besides you, knows the full extent of your daily suffering. And He cares. He's working for the good of those who love Him.

This might be a good time to invite Jesus to walk out and shout to your personal storm, "Silence! Be still!" Accept the reality of grace, of your own acceptance by God. Sure, things may still boggle your mind, and you may still struggle with questions, but the presence of Christ will guide you even amid the suffering.

Chapter 6

LOVE BOUND BY PROMISE

God's perspective on us is remarkable, almost unbelievable. He delights in us and loves us as a caring Father. He's running toward us, ready to embrace and forgive us. He's for us in all the pain of life and can sustain us in every challenge.

As I learn to see from God's perspective, my perspective on everything else shifts. I realize that my failures don't disqualify me. I'm aware of the security I already have in God's grace. I trust that nothing will separate me from the love of God in Christ.

Yet there are still times when I am tempted to question and wrestle with fear. Does God really see me as His forgiven child? Even if He forgave my past, what about my future blowouts? Will God be faithful to me when I am faithless? Thankfully, God addresses these questions with a promise.

When my son was three and a half, we took the family to Disneyland. He had been there before, but this was the first time he cleared the minimum height requirements for most rides—by a quarter inch. We were fired up! So I immediately took him on Space Mountain, which is a pretty good-sized roller coaster. It runs inside a huge dark outcropping of rock with strobe lights flashing and music blaring. It's a lot for a little guy to handle.

After we sat down, I could see some fear in Ethan's eyes. I didn't just say, "Ethan, even though you're so small that the seat bar won't fully come down to your waist, and even though you're so short that you can't see anything but the back of the seat in front of you, and even though we're going to fly through the dark at fifty miles an hour to the sound of the Red Hot Chili Peppers jamming, with lights flashing, don't be afraid." That would've been crazy.

> Sometimes life is big-time frightening. We're going at warp speed, flying totally in the dark. We don't have a clue what's coming next, and everything around us is chaotic.

No. I said, "Ethan, don't be afraid, because Daddy's got you. I'll hold you, and I promise I won't let anything happen to you."

That promise made the difference. Ethan nodded his little head and clung to the lap bar for dear life. The coaster took off, and I had to hold his head up on the turns because he was all over that seat. When we finally came to the end, I was proud of him.

I said, "Son, you did an awesome job. What did you think?"

"Scawy, Dad," he said. "That was scawy."

Sometimes life *is* scawy. Big-time frightening. We're going at warp speed, flying totally in the dark. We don't have a clue what's coming next, and everything around us is chaotic.

But God doesn't just say, "Don't be afraid." He makes a promise that He'll always be there, that He's our helper and we can depend on Him.

The book of Hebrews describes God's amazing promise. God says, "I will never fail you. I will never abandon you."[1] The promise is followed by a response: "So we can say with confidence, 'The LORD is my helper, so I will have no fear. What can mere people do to me?'"[2]

In a sense, the promise—"I will never abandon you"—is more about God than it is about us. It declares His faithfulness to His covenant.

Today, if I had a piece of land that came right up against your piece of land, and if we didn't want each other to come onto our respective properties, we'd just put up a fence. The way they did it in the ancient world was different—*way* different. If two people wanted to come to an understanding between themselves, they would make a covenant, or a spiritual agreement. And they would seal it with a pretty gory ritual.

First they would take some animals and cut each animal in half lengthwise. Then they would separate the pieces of each animal. And each party to the agreement would walk between the pieces. It was a solemn ceremony, a little weird by modern-day tastes, but it definitely got the participants' attention. Here's what each party was effectively saying by walking through the animal pieces: "May God do this to me [what had happened to the animals] if I break this covenant."

Now, God came to Abraham and said these words: "Do not be afraid...for I will protect you."[3] Then God promised that Abraham would possess the land of Israel and would be blessed. Abraham had this promise, but he didn't have much to show for it. So God had him get a ram, a goat, a heifer, a turtledove, and a young pigeon.

Abraham separated the pieces of the larger animals. He and God were apparently going to walk through the pieces to establish the ultimate covenant between God and humankind.

God was guaranteeing His promise to Abraham. He would bless Abraham—and through him, the entire world, including believers in generations yet to come. Talk about a pivotal point in history! This was one of the huge ones.

But there was one big hitch. God couldn't swear by anybody higher than Himself. He didn't need old Abe to walk through the pieces with Him. So what He did was have Abraham fall into a deep sleep. Instead of Abraham walking through the pieces, he now was catching ZZZs. And God alone passed between the pieces.

Why is this significant?

Because God was binding Himself to *Himself.* Who else can God swear by who's higher than He is? Nobody! He's God. He and Abraham could have made a joint covenant, but with Abe being human, what surely would have happened at some point was that Abe would have failed to hold up his end of the deal. So God effectively said, "I'm going to swear by Myself."

> The deal is that if you have entered by faith into an agreement with God through Christ, He is bound by His own character to be there for you.

God made a covenant with Abraham. He made another, even more important covenant, through Jesus and His death on the cross—a covenant promising that all who follow Jesus will be accepted by the Father and will live with God forever. He locked up the promise with the covenant.

The Bible says, "We have this hope as an anchor for the soul, firm and secure."[4] The assurance, in other words, is that God will be faithful to us because He has bound Himself to Himself.

The deal is that if you have entered by faith into this agreement with God through Christ, He is bound by His own character to be there for you. You and He have a covenant. He's not going to back out of it. He has promised by His very nature to be with you all the time in the midst of your stuff.

He'll be with you when it gets *scawy*.

A while back I had a chance to hang out with Paulie Teutul Jr. from Orange County Choppers when he agreed to speak at Central. His family's television program, *American Chopper,* is a reality show that airs each week on The Learning Channel. It airs in 160 countries and is expanding rapidly. The motorcycle world has never seen a show like it.

Paulie is down-to-earth and real, and we all found his story compelling. He grew up in an alcoholic home until he was ten. He spent a lot of that time afraid. He feared his dad, feared going to school, feared what would happen to his family. Because he was the oldest child, he felt responsible for the family. Once his dad sobered up, Paul Sr. became involved in his life, but it took some time for things to heal.

Paulie became a Christian at age twelve as a result of his mother's influence. She took the family to church, taught them, and challenged them.

But even though he was a Christian, Paulie still went through two seasons of heavy partying in his younger years. One landed him in rehab at sixteen. Another continued into his midtwenties.

One day, in his midtwenties, he had what he calls a nervous breakdown. Anxiety, fear, and depression overwhelmed him. He couldn't function anymore and had to spend time in a hospital. He continued to wrestle with anxiety and depression in intense ways for another year.

He credits his faith in God and the church for getting him through this tough phase in his life. In time, he jumped into serving in his local church, volunteering in the men's ministry and as an usher. He spent three nights a week at church doing all he could to grow. He talked about the power of the Bible in his life and the huge impact prayer had made for him. He said Jesus filled the place in his soul that nothing else could fill. God allowed Paul to face his fears.

> God's work in our lives is messy, and sometimes life feels chaotic. Even there, God meets us. He shows up even when things get terrifying.

Yes, God's work in our lives is messy, and sometimes life feels chaotic. Even there, God meets us. He shows up even when things get terrifying. He has bound Himself to the promise that He will never leave us. So we can take up the response: "The LORD is my helper, so I will have no fear. What can mere people do to me?"[5]

When I'm afraid, when I'm wrestling with fear before a confrontation I'm about to have or a situation I'm dreading, I remind myself of this confession. I whisper it over and over, or I run it through my mind again and again. After a few minutes, I find that a great peace settles in and I'm empowered to face my current challenge.

You may be afraid today of really facing the truth about what's going on in your life.

Maybe it's an addiction. *The LORD is my helper, so I will have no fear.*

Maybe you're afraid today of the direction in which your marriage is headed. *The LORD is my helper, so I will have no fear.*

Maybe you're single and time is running out and you're afraid you'll never be married. *The LORD is my helper, so I will have no fear.*

Maybe you and your spouse have tried again and again to start a family, but the pregnancy tests keep coming back negative and you're afraid you'll never have kids. *The LORD is my helper, so I will have no fear.*

Perhaps you're facing a job change that is terrifying to you. *The LORD is my helper, so I will have no fear.*

Perhaps you have a spouse or child who serves in the armed forces and you're afraid he or she might never come home. *The LORD is my helper, so I will have no fear.*

Maybe you're up against the question of having to take care of your parents each day—a potentially life-changing obligation—or putting them in a nursing home. *The LORD is my helper, so I will have no fear.*

Whatever you're up against, remember God's promise. He will never fail you and never abandon you. And take up the response. He is your helper, so have no fear.

Part 2

WIDE OPEN TO IDENTITY

Chapter 7

SMASH YOUR MIRROR

In junior high, I spent way too much time looking in the mirror. Some of this time involved checking zits and acne—every teen's nightmare. I always walked to the mirror with some dread, not knowing what new thing would've appeared on my face. But I spent more time in front of my mirror playing air guitar to the blaring music of rock bands. I would daydream that I was the rock star and the crowd was swooning in awe of me. If one of my parents walked in, of course, I'd quickly go from jamming on my air guitar to bending down like I was tying my shoe. What I saw in that mirror was a long way from being the real me.

Mirrors don't always tell the truth. Just ask David Copperfield. Several nights a week he does things like walk through a seven-foot-high, five-inch-thick plate-glass mirror he has just shown his audience. He walks through it and then shows that it's still standing there, as solid as it was before.

Copperfield—tall, wearing flowing long white sleeves and black tuxedo pants—can do anything with mirrors. Maybe his most amazing illusion is called Origami.

He comes out on stage holding an Oriental-style box about two feet long on every side. He places the box on a low table with a huge mirror behind it so that the audience can see the reflection of everything that's happening. He then takes three four-foot-long samurai swords and intersects the box with them up, down, and sideways. The audience is already spellbound.

Then a beautiful woman joins the illusionist on stage. They caress each other for a while, moving about the stage as sensuous music plays in the background. Copperfield then removes the swords and unfolds the box origami-style to make it barely large enough for the woman to climb into. At his bidding, she does so, folding herself tightly into the box.

Copperfield closes the top and retrieves the three swords. With appropriate flourishes, he again pierces the box with the swords up, down, and sideways. After this, he withdraws the swords from the box and places them on a rack (the audience is half looking for blood on them after what they've just seen). Then he carefully opens the box and—voilà!—the girl slowly unfolds herself and climbs out, embracing Copperfield as the romantic music plays.

How does he do it? It's all in the mirror, I suspect. But David Copperfield is never going to tell.

Our identity comes down to mirrors as well. In part 1, we looked at how God sees us. We talked about the importance of grace and of accepting that we are children of God, standing in His grace, covered in His love, and secure in His promise. But we also need to face the truth of our self-image. Too often our view is distorted.

When you look in the mirror, what do you see? If you're like most people, your first tendency is to notice what's wrong with your hair. Or to cut yourself down because of the bulge at your waist. Or because your ears stick out too much. (One major-league baseball player's ears stuck out so much that his teammates said he looked like a taxicab speeding downhill with its doors open.) You might say to yourself, *Why do I have such squinty eyes?* Or, *Wow, I can't believe this! There's actually hair growing out of my ears.*

But how about the "mirror" that is your self-image? When you think about yourself, what do you see on the inside? Is the image distorted? Is the reflection more of your past experiences than of your new spiritual identity? Is the image reflective of God's view of you? Our view of ourselves in this kind of "mirror" is often one in which we focus on our negative points, just as we do when we look in an actual mirror.

A friend of mine named Tammy looks like the average girl next door, with her black hair and long-sleeve shirts. But Tammy has been through a lot of pain. She was sexually abused by her father and then later by a youth pastor when she was a teen. She took it out on her body by having tattoos etched on every square inch of her skin except her face, neck, and hands. She says the tattoos were to cover the pain she saw when she looked in the mirror.

> When you think about yourself, what do you see on the inside? Is the reflection more of your past experiences than of your new spiritual identity?

As you can imagine, Tammy had a lot of trust issues with pastors and stayed away from church for a long time. I consider it a real honor that she came to trust me and allowed me to be a pastor to her. She is a special person who is an encouragement to many. What allowed Tammy to change was seeing herself through God's Word. It became like a new mirror for her that transformed her identity.

James got at this amazing power that resides in living out God's Word when he wrote, "If you listen to the word and don't obey, it is like glancing at your face in a mirror. You see yourself, walk away, and forget what you look like. But if you look carefully into the perfect law that sets you free, and if you do what it says and don't forget what you heard, then God will bless you for doing it."[1]

> This is the truth of the mirror: If you consistently see yourself as worthless, you will start to behave in a manner that corresponds with that belief. If you see yourself as an accepted follower of Christ, that will affect how you behave as well.

Catch that? If we merely read God's Word and don't obey it, it's as if we forget what we look like. But if we read and obey, we see ourselves as we are—children of God, loved by Him. We experience the law that sets us free.

This perfect law does not start with our behavior—our performance before God and the world. It starts with believing we are who God says we are.

People often ask me how I can be a pastor in a town like Las Vegas. And doing so would be tough, I suppose, if I just looked at people's behavior as the problem. But I don't see behavior as the core issue most of the time. It is an issue, but it is usually a symptom of something else. I often find belief to be more of a core issue. As people's beliefs about God and themselves change, their behavior tends to follow.

Neil Anderson puts it this way: "No person can consistently behave in a way that's inconsistent with the way he perceives himself."[2] It goes back to the truth of the mirror. If you consistently see yourself as worthless, you will start to behave in a manner that corresponds with that belief. If you see yourself as an accepted follower of Christ, forgiven by grace, that will affect how you behave as well.

Cindy viewed herself as virtually unforgivable and irreparable. She reinforced this belief in many ways, one of which was a drug addiction. In the ups and downs of her addiction, she desperately wanted to change, but she was also terrified of changing. She would attend church to hear of God's love and find some hope, but she felt so bad about herself that she couldn't muster the courage to get sober. So she would often get high before she showed up for church. She would sit in the section farthest from the front and effectively hide out from most of the others who attended.

One weekend we showed a video of a woman named Sara who talked about how she would take several shots of alcohol before she could get up enough courage to come to church alone and sit in the last row. After doing this for a long time, she had eventually surrendered her life to God and began the transformation process that has resulted in more than eight years of sobriety.

As Cindy watched this video, she saw herself.

That weekend I challenged the attendees to get honest with another person and to get honest with God about what was going on in their lives. And so, after the service, Cindy went to an information area at our church and talked to a friend named Joan.

"You know what?" Cindy said. "That woman on the video might as well be me. That's what I've been doing. I need God in my life, and I need a new start."

Joan didn't judge her. She put her arm around Cindy and gave her the information she needed for the next steps in her life. Cindy wrote about it:

> That day, Christ set me free and filled my once-empty heart.
> I know now that my way hadn't worked for the past twelve
> years. I decided to do it God's way from now on. I finally
> found that the purpose I had been searching after for so long
> was Jesus. I'm sober now. I'm not alone anymore. I have
> peace. I'm coming to church and working through recovery.
> I'm whole again. I no longer live by my will but by Christ's
> will for my life.

Over time, Cindy completely changed how she saw herself. She broke the mirror that had once portrayed her as worthless and afraid.

Many of us need to do the same. We need to break the mirror we've been looking at.

A lot of superstitions are connected with mirrors. The most pervasive superstition seems to be that when you break a mirror, you're automatically facing seven years of bad luck. But the kind of mirror breaking I'm talking about can bring all kinds of good, not bad, into our lives. Cindy and many others can attest to this.

Many of us need to break the mirror we've been looking at.

The real hex in our lives is not in the mirror but in how we see ourselves in it. Maybe it's time for you to smash the mirror that doesn't reflect your new identity in Christ.

Chapter 8

YOUR NEW ID

One of the places I despise most is the Department of Motor Vehicles. At the DMV, everybody is in a bad mood. There usually aren't enough places to park. The lines are endless. And the besieged clerks, some of whom apparently stopped talking when they joined the DMV, have faraway looks in their eyes.

It seems to be the same at every DMV office, in every state. The soul-sapping boredom of such places is hardly news. But a few years ago the DMV in North Las Vegas actually made national headlines.

In the middle of the night, burglars rammed a Hummer or some other heavy-duty vehicle through a back wall of the DMV, worked their way through the place, and made off with seventeen hundred blank Nevada driver's licenses as well as the equipment to print faces and names on them. Worse, the thieves also stole a hard drive that contained the social security numbers and other personal information for more than eight thousand people who had valid driver's licenses.[1]

There's hardly anything in the realm of sin that hasn't happened in Las Vegas before, but this smash-through was a new one. It raised the potential of massive identity theft, not to mention a homeland security threat.

But I've got still worse news for you: You don't have to have your bank accounts emptied and your license ripped off to lose your identity. You can just as easily lose your identity in a relationship, in the cloud of a past mistake. You can lose it in success, in a job, in an addiction, or even in a hobby. There are all sorts of identity thieves out there that would love to drain your life.

Too many of us are walking around as if we've had our identity stolen. We're worn out and tired. We've lost the spark for life we once had. We've wound down…and d-o-w-n…and d…o…w…n until there's not much life left.

We need to open our eyes wide to our true identity.

The Bible has a lot to say about our identity. For example, Peter wrote, "You are a *chosen* people. You are *royal* priests, a *holy* nation, *God's very own* possession. As a result, you can show others the goodness of God, for *he called you* out of the darkness into his wonderful light. 'Once you had no identity as a people; now you are God's people. Once you received no mercy; now you have received God's mercy.'"[2]

> Our identity is now found in God—not in our pursuits, not in the way we act, but in Him.

Peter was talking about our collective identity as Christians, but this also is a message to us as individuals. Before it dawned on us that Jesus Christ is real and is willing to live in our hearts, many of us were lost in our personal identity crises. But as we become followers of Jesus, the

Bible says, we take on a new identity as God's people. Our identity is now found in Him—not in our pursuits, not in the way we act, but in Him.

If somebody asked me, "Who are you?" I could say lots of things. I could say, "I am Jud. I am married to Lori. We have two kids and a slobbery bulldog named Roxy. And I am horrible at Guitar Hero for Xbox."

These are aspects of who I am, but my identity is not found in them. According to the Bible, my identity is found in God. He chooses me. I'm His possession. And that is who you are too.

It doesn't matter what your employer says, what your parents say, what your ex says, or what your friends say. God says that as His follower you are chosen.

It doesn't matter what your employer says, what your parents say, what your ex says, or what your friends say. God says that as His follower you are chosen. You are loved just as you are, and your identity is complete in that. You can't earn it, and you can't undo it; there is nothing you can do to achieve it. What could be more awesome?

We're talking about cosmic stuff here. Maybe that's why the apostle Paul exploded with thanks and praise in the opening of a letter he wrote to the church at Ephesus. It's as if he was so relieved and excited to be chosen by God that he couldn't hold back. He wrote, "All praise to God, the Father of our Lord Jesus Christ, who has blessed us with every spiritual blessing in the heavenly realms because we are united with Christ. Even before he made the world, God loved us and chose us in Christ."[3]

Think about this for a moment. It's staggering. God has chosen us—all who believe—to be part of His team. He's saying that each of us, as a follower of Jesus, has made the cut. And not only that, but we were also first-round draft picks. Actually, we were chosen before the draft even started. We were chosen from the foundations of the world.

The only thing Paul knew to do in light of this was to give thanks. He all but freaked out through the first fourteen verses of his letter to the Ephesians. Most of it is one garbled run-on sentence. He talked about how believers in Christ were chosen before the beginning of the world to be holy and blameless in God's sight, how we are blessed in the heavenly realms, how our freedom was purchased by the blood of Jesus, how we are adopted through Jesus and showered with kindness and wisdom. And you get the sense that Paul could have gone on and on if he had let himself. He was in awe of the God who had chosen him.

Living in one of the entertainment hot spots of the world, I'm always getting asked for tickets to different concerts and shows by visiting friends. Everybody wants a freebie to the latest big thing. Sometimes I can help, but there are a few shows I can't do anything about.

One of these was the Céline Dion show at Caesars Palace. I might have been able to work over some friends and get tickets at face value when the show was sold out, but there were never any freebies to Céline. She was just too popular.

By 2007, the famous willowy Canadian singer had performed at more than seven hundred sellout shows over a five-year period. Night after night, she had filled the 4,100-seat coliseum at Caesars—an unbelievable theater with a 120-foot-wide and 60-foot-high stage. She had appeared before nearly three million people and had grossed a staggering $385 million.

So you can imagine that when Céline told Caesars that she would be leaving in 2008, the famously opulent hotel on the Strip had a major problem on its hands.

Caesars's president had to hire her replacement, and it had to be someone who could fill Céline's big shoes. After all, Vegas is Vegas. You need a name if you're Caesars Palace. So what he did to keep packing them in at the coliseum was to woo Bette Midler, the Divine Miss M.

Of the hundreds of stars he could have considered, he *chose* Bette Midler. Now, as someone not from Bette's generation, I have no idea why. Of all the people he could have chosen, Bette Midler? Hello? But I was not the one doing the choosing. That was Caesars's prerogative even when it made no sense to me.

The same is true for God. I've often wondered, *Why in the world would God choose me?* I imagine those who knew me in my past would say, "This is crazy." But the fact is, He chose me, and He chose you, for His glory. It is His prerogative, and it doesn't have to make sense to us.

"Even before he made the world," the Bible says, *"God loved us* and chose us in Christ to be holy and without fault in his eyes."[4]

Now, Christians have struggled for generations over what being chosen really means. It's one of the great mysteries in Christianity. I appreciate the perspective that says that before you become a Christian there's a door with this message above it: "Enter here all who will choose to believe." You can enter or just stroll by. But if you do enter, when you turn around, over the door on the inside are the words "Chosen from the foundations of the world."

In other words, God's choosing and our choosing are not irreconcilable. God is God, and there's much we don't fully understand when we're still this side of heaven. But the important thing is that if we've gone through that door, we now live in awe and wonder because we have been picked by God.

He chose us, regardless of what we would do in our lives, regardless of our lustful thoughts, regardless of our tendency to cheat and cut corners and put ourselves forward as number one. He chose us to love Him and be His children and representatives on this earth.

This idea of choosing should lead us not to confusion and theological warfare but to our knees in awe and wonder before God.

One beautiful thing about life is that you just never know whom God will choose and who will choose Him.

As a kid growing up, I was a huge fan of Evel Knievel. I played with my Evel Knievel toy motorcycle set and created elaborate "jumps" down the hallway of our home.

I remember watching Evel's final jumps as a young boy. Each time, I was nervous that he wouldn't make the jump. I can still sense my fear for him, which also oozed out of my parents as we sat before the TV. And I danced for joy when he landed on the other side.

Later, when I moved to Las Vegas, I found Evel to be part of the town's history. He's almost as synonymous with Vegas as Elvis or Wayne Newton. Part of his appeal was that he was a common guy who conquered the odds against him.

On December 31, 1967, Evel captivated the nation (thereby helping Las Vegas become what it has turned out to be) by speeding off a ramp and soaring on his motorcycle 151 feet over the majestic fountains of Caesars Palace, "only to land in a spectacular bone-breaking crash."[5] His rag-doll somersault from the bike left him in a coma for twenty-nine days with a shattered pelvis, broken hip, and smashed right femur. Surgeons rebuilt his leg with a nearly two-foot-long, three-inch-wide steel bar.

Evel was hard living, with craggy good looks, a tight white leather suit, and the bottom of his pant legs flaring out over white leather cowboy boots. He was a folk hero of sorts, and for a while he was on the short list of the most famous people in America.

> He chose us, regardless of what we would do in our lives, regardless of our lustful thoughts, regardless of our tendency to cheat and cut corners and put ourselves forward as number one. He chose us to love Him and be His children.

A one-time safecracker, bank robber, and miner, Evel never shied from a challenge. In 1973, zooming on his motorcycle down a ski jump before takeoff, he made his best jump by clearing fifty-two cars packed side to side in the Los Angeles Coliseum. Another time, he jumped over thirteen double-decker buses parked side by side at Wembley Stadium in London, breaking his pelvis in the process.

In 1974, Evel launched himself on a rocket across the Snake River Canyon in Idaho as the world looked on via network TV. But a parachute deployed from his rocket on takeoff, and he landed back on the same side of the canyon he had taken off from, blood seeping from his ears and eyes because of the g-force.[6]

Knievel once said, "The guy who built Caesars Palace once told me I was the biggest gambler Vegas had ever seen because I didn't gamble with money. I gambled with my life."

Another time he told an interviewer, "People said I wasn't scared before a jump.... I *was* scared. I'd have a shot of Wild Turkey whiskey before each jump to calm myself.... People who go around wearing 'No Fear' T-shirts are full of [it].... If you risk your life you have got to have fear."[7]

The toll on Evel's body, which he loved bragging about, was horrific. He repeatedly shattered bones as well as bikes. There's an entry under his name in the *Guinness Book of World Records* for "Most Broken Bones, Lifetime: 35." When he was forced to retire in 1980 at age forty-one, he told reporters he was "nothing but scar tissue and surgical steel."[8]

He told the *New York Times* he had undergone fifteen major operations to relieve severe trauma and repair broken bones—skull, pelvis, ribs, collarbone, femur, shoulders, and hips. "I created the character called Evel Knievel, and he sort of got away from me," he said in what may have been the most insightful comment of his life.

"He had a titanium hip and aluminum plates in his arms and a great many pins holding other bones and joints together," the *Times* said upon his death in December 2007. "He was in so many accidents that he occasionally broke some of his metal parts, too."[9]

To deal with the pain and get his body to move again, he washed down painkillers with an Evel cocktail he named the Montana Mary, after his home state—take a can of beer, a can of tomato juice, as many shots of Wild Turkey as you like, shake it up…and put it down.

Blood tainted with hepatitis C was used during one of the surgeries that pieced him back together. That caused massive hemorrhaging inside his neck and led to a liver transplant that eventually slowed him down. But for decades outside the public eye, Evel lived like a rock star on steroids. In the 1970s and 1980s, Evel Knievel toys had sales in the hundreds of millions of dollars.

As for the women, he estimated at age sixty-one that he had slept with two thousand of them. "I had about two a week," he told one writer. "My record was eight in one 24-hour period. It got to be a real problem. I had to see a psychiatrist."[10]

After illness forced Evel to leave the national stage in the 1980s, he lost much of the fortune he had amassed. Gone were the five Rolls-Royces. Gone were the five Ferraris, the Lamborghini, and the two jet airplanes. He loved the airplanes so much that he had them flown alongside each other on his trips so he could read his name on the side. Yeah, Evel Knievel!

Eventually, Evel's wife of many years, Linda, left him. By early 2007, she had been praying for almost thirty years for him to come to

Christ, and she even had her church in Butte, Montana, interceding for him. Unknown to him, Evel's daughter also had her church in Bozeman, Montana, praying for him.

On April 22, 2007, those who tuned in to the weekly *Hour of Power* TV broadcast were surprised to see Robert Schuller, the eighty-year-old televised pastor, introducing Evel Knievel to his audience. Knievel was a plain-spoken gray-haired man who looked nothing like the swashbuckling, leather-suited icon of decades past.

"I never thought that I would be here," Evel said on the air. "I just was a person who always believed that there was a God power, but I always had trouble believing in Jesus Christ, the Son of God. I don't know why I fought it so hard. I just did.…

"I think maybe it was the power of prayer, maybe God just got sick and tired of me fighting it so much. So He reached out and grabbed me and said, 'Look, Evel, you've got to stop this nonsense, You just come to Me.…'

"So I don't know what in the world happened. I don't know if it was the power of prayer, or God Himself, which was reaching me while I was driving or walking down the sidewalk or sleeping. The power of God in Jesus just grabbed me! It just took a hold of me. It was so strong. I can't tell you how strong it was.… All of a sudden I just believed in Jesus Christ. I did! I believed in Him!"[11]

I was fascinated to hear Evel Knievel talking about God choosing him and about his own response. But as he talked to the world of his security in Christ, no one knew that nine months later, on November 30, 2007, Evel Knievel would pass away at age sixty-nine.

For years he'd had a tombstone, plot, and funeral plans already in place, but in the last year of his life he made a significant adjustment. He had the words "Believe in Jesus Christ" inscribed on his tombstone. They remain there today as a reminder to all to embrace a new identity as a chosen child of God.

Chapter 9

BE A SAINT

Here's a statement that might shock you: It doesn't matter if you feel like a saint or even act like a saint. As a follower of Jesus, *you already are one.* It is part of your new identity.

We've been learning how our view of God affects how we see ourselves. Our identity is no longer found in our stuff or in our jobs. We now see ourselves as people loved and accepted by God, chosen by Him. But it gets even better—we are also saints.

In the aftermath of Hurricane Katrina in 2005, many wondered if New Orleans would rise again. The city's pain had America transfixed. In a certain sense, that fall we were a nation of New Orleanians, such was the heartache that bound us together.

As the rebuilding began, one of the biggest milestones was the opening of the refurbished Superdome, home of the New Orleans Saints football team. Their first game in the new dome was unbelievable. Not only did they play inspired football, but the performances by U2 and Green Day were also over the top. The musicians played "The Saints Are Coming," and the place went nuts.

The slogan I heard again and again around the game was "Be a Saint." Thousands of people wore T-shirts with the slogan. Players challenged us on commercials to "Be a Saint." It was a great thing for the city and a strong message for our nation.

When I hear this exhortation to "Be a Saint," I realize again how transformative the Bible's message really is. The Bible's teaching isn't simply to "be a saint" but to realize that you already are one and to live out of that.

Paul addressed his letters to several churches with the words "to the saints." He didn't intend for the letters to be read only to the religious elite but rather was calling all those who followed Christ "saints," even if they were imperfect.

Churches in those days were hardly prettier than they are today. Some of them were filled with gossip, backbiting, partying, sexual immorality, and lawsuits. Yet Paul still called the members of those churches "saints" because that was their position before God.

> The Bible's teaching isn't simply to "be a saint" but to realize that you already are one and to live out of that.

In Ephesians he said that God has reconciled people to Himself through the cross and has made peace. He told his readers, "You are no longer strangers and aliens, but you are fellow citizens with the *saints,* and are of God's household."[1]

Now, think about this for a moment. It is amazing that God forgives us, but He also gives us the status of righteousness *now.*

The Bible actually presents two realities: an experiential reality and a positional one. Experientially, I still fail. I don't always act like a saint. I lose my temper or compromise God's standard. But positionally, I'm a saint. I'm forgiven and made right by the grace of God. I don't have to fight for reconciliation or strive to achieve it. All I need to do is see it and accept it.

This came home to me most powerfully one summer when I was on break from college. I had been spending a lot of time trying to reconcile the fact that I am a sinner with the fact that God says I'm a saint. I struggled with all my might to "be a saint." I had periods of great effort. Times where I'd spend days in prayer and fasting. I'd devour my Bible and serve others. But through it all I still felt like I'd never measure up with God. I wasn't all that saintly, no matter how much I tried.

> It is amazing that God forgives us, but He also gives us the status of righteousness *now*.

That summer I dedicated a lot of time to reading and praying through this tension in my life. I saw that living out of my position in Christ is first about knowing, not doing. Paul wrote, "We *know* that our old sinful selves were crucified with Christ so that sin might lose its power in our lives."[2]

What we know is that we have been crucified with Christ. Our sinful nature has been put to death. We don't have to do anything to cause this to happen. We don't have to work and sweat and strive for what we already have. We merely must come to a place where we "know" it. This knowing isn't book knowledge but is knowing in our hearts that God has forgiven us. Knowing that all our human effort won't make any difference. We accept God's forgiveness and live out of that day by day.

Hudson Taylor was a remarkable missionary to China in the nineteenth century. Yet despite all his achievements, he still struggled with his own sin and unworthiness. He felt that if he could only abide in Christ, he would be free from the shackles of guilt and remorse.

One day he experienced a life-changing realization that his freedom in Christ would not be because of all his striving or effort to "abide" in Christ but instead would come from simply remembering that he already *did* abide in Him.

Writing to his sister, he said,

> I do not know how far I may be able to make myself intelligible about it, for there is nothing new or strange or wonderful— and yet, all is new! In a word, "whereas once I was blind, now I see."… I am dead and buried with Christ—aye, and risen too and ascended…. God reckons me so, and tells me to reckon myself so. He knows best…. Oh, the joy of seeing this truth— I do pray that the eyes of your understanding may be enlightened, that you may know and enjoy the riches freely given us in Christ.[3]

That summer on break from college, I experienced what Hudson Taylor had written about. I began to realize that the way I would overcome sin in my own life was not first by effort. I had tried that. It was by knowing that God had already done it in my life. Rather than constantly praying for help in a certain area of my life, I began to thank God for already delivering me from that area "in Christ." I began to live out of my new identity "in Christ." In general, I stopped trying so hard and started thanking God for His effort. I began to live more out of gratitude than out of guilt. Grace finally was flowing into my heart and life, but it all began by having my eyes opened, with knowing.

Another aspect of realizing we're saints is believing. Paul continued, "So you also should consider yourselves to be dead to the power of sin and alive to God through Christ Jesus."[4] He was saying we should believe that we are dead to sin and alive to God. Every time I had read this passage in the past, I immediately jumped to the phrase "dead to the power of sin." I knew I was anything but, so I would try harder. But that summer I saw for the first time that Paul was saying we are already dead to the power of sin, so we should believe ourselves to be so. We should live out of the reality God has already established.

It is like when Jesus says, "Abide in me."[5] I immediately think, *Okay, what are all the things I need to do to get to a place of abiding?* But Jesus was saying, in essence, "You already abide in Me. God has already placed you there. Now simply believe it and remain there."

This sounds crazy. *Consider yourselves dead to sin even though you are not!* But this considering is where we place our faith and trust in God's Word. This is seeing ourselves as God sees us. This is believing, in spite of evidence to the contrary, that God has delivered us from the power of sin.

As we know and believe this, then we "present [ourselves] to God as being alive from the dead, and [our] members as instruments of righteousness to God."[6] It isn't simply that we present ourselves before God, but that we present ourselves "as being alive from the dead." Each day we give ourselves to Him, we surrender our will, we live as servants for God's purpose. Precisely because of our position in Christ, we are motivated to live holy lives. God does care how we live and what we do. Understanding my position in Christ helped me live more like Christ. I strive harder to be holy, not out of guilt and misconstrued fear, but out of thankfulness and joy.

Sure, there are times when I experientially fail, but this doesn't change my position. My standing is a gift from God. I'm a saint, and so are you.

The person who has helped me understand this most is author and teacher Brennan Manning. I'll never forget the day I met Brennan. I didn't know much about him at the time, but a friend invited me to a breakfast with him. Immediately I was struck by this man who had such a presence of compassion. He took a few hours to share his story and insights. I sat mesmerized.

Brennan was ordained a priest in 1963 and taught theology at the University of Steubenville in Ohio. Later he joined a spiritual group in Spain for two years and worked among the poor. He then spent time as a missionary to a Swiss prison, where the only person who knew he was not actually a prisoner was the warden. He said that if the prisoners had known he was a priest, he wouldn't have been able to really minister to them. For more than ten years he poured his life out for the poor. At one period he lived on a trash heap with the poorest of the poor in Mexico. After his time spent in

Europe and South America, he came back to the United States and served a campus ministry at a community college.

And then something went wrong. This theology professor, priest, and servant began drinking heavily. He began to serve the bottle. Eventually he found himself homeless, sleeping in a gutter— a drunk. He wanted to say, "Lord, I've failed, and I can never serve You again."

He realized he had three options: insanity, death, or sobriety. So, thankfully, he got honest about his failures, accepted God's grace, and sought help. After six months in treatment, he was released.

In one of my favorite books, *The Ragamuffin Gospel,* he says, "Often I have been asked, 'Brennan, how is it possible that you became an alcoholic after you got saved?' It is possible because I got battered and bruised by loneliness and failure; because I got discouraged, uncertain, guilt-ridden, and took my eyes off Jesus. Because the Christ-encounter did not transfigure me into an angel."[7]

As I listened to Brennan, I was inspired by this person radically changed by God's grace. His books sell well and his speaking schedule is full, but what impresses me the most is his humility. He

> Next time you look in the mirror, say hello to your true identity: saint.

already knew when and where the local Alcoholics Anonymous meeting was in our city, and he planned to go. There he would sit in a circle with others, where it doesn't matter what your résumé says. There he would sit as a saint with a strong appetite for beer who was saved by the grace of God.

Maybe you've got the sin part down but not the saint part. Next time you look in the mirror, say hello to your true identity: saint. If you have received God's grace through Jesus Christ, you are a saint. Then set about in your day to reflect in every way and to every person your new standing in the eyes of God. You're no angel. But you're something even more astonishing. You're truly "alive from the dead." You're now and forever a saint.

Chapter 10

Priests
Without Collars

I've been called a lot of things, but one of the oddest sounding is "priest." The first time someone called me a priest, I actually looked behind me to see if they were referring to someone else. But the amazing thing is that all Christ followers are called "priests."

We've noted that our new identity impacts our self-image. Rather than see ourselves through the lenses of failure or our past or our parents, we see ourselves according to God's Word. We each have a special position in Christ *now*. We are already saints "in Him," and we are also priests, even without collars.

My friend Heather Veitch takes her role as a priest to an unlikely group of people—adult dancers.

Heather grew up in a poor neighborhood in California, where she was raised by her single mom. Her mom tried to be there for her as best she could, but Heather, who was quite pretty but without well-defined boundaries, was often alone. She was raped for the first time at fourteen years old and again by the time she was sixteen.

Heather led a life of promiscuity in high school and became pregnant at seventeen. She missed a lot of school, did her best to catch up, and was able to graduate. A short while later, looking to do the right thing for her son, she got married to someone other than the boy's father. It was difficult from the get-go. Her husband was controlling, constantly challenging her, and impossible to deal with, so before long she took her son and left him.

The husband, emotionally unstable, attempted suicide three times and eventually began stalking her. By this point Heather was working two jobs, at a restaurant by day and a nightclub by night. Once, in the wee hours of the morning, she came home to find that her husband, in a move that only a twisted mind could conceive, had cut all her clothes in two.

Fearing for her life, she told her bosses what had happened, took her son to her grandmother's, and moved to San Francisco in search of a job. And the first one she could find that paid well was as a nightclub dancer.

A short while later she retrieved her son and moved to Southern California, where she got a job as a bikini dancer. Talented and better looking than most girls in the business, she kept advancing in the dance industry until she was doing topless and then nude dancing. She was making good money for the first time, shuttling between California and Las Vegas.

By 1998, the millennium was approaching—and with it apocalyptic fears of computer networks crashing and the end of the world drawing nigh. It wasn't the first time Heather had feared death, but for the first time a thought occurred to her: *If the world does end, will I die as a dancer and go to hell?*

The thought was persistent. Persistent to the point that she started bargaining with God. "I don't want to die yet," she told Him, "so please keep me alive long enough that I can change."

She partied her brains out well into 1999, when she wasn't stripping, and attended beauty school to prepare for a possible long-term career. But the signal event of that year was that she gave her life fully and without reservation to Christ. She also got married to her live-in boyfriend and finally made a full break from stripping.

As Heather describes it, she became a rude and judgmental Christian over the next several years. She had left her past behind her, but she wasn't acting as a priest to a broken world. Then in 2005 she learned that a stripper friend of hers, with whom she used to drink, had died from alcoholism. Realizing it easily could have been her, Heather kept asking herself, *Why not me?*

After the funeral, she went out to the cemetery and stood by the tombstone. She thought about this friend and all the things she was caught up in when she died. Heather says she realized that she was too comfortable. God was calling her to step out and do something.

Heather saw that many sex clubs *used* young women, while few if any *cared* for them. She began praying that God would reveal what she could do to help these women. She increasingly began to sense that God was telling her to go back to the clubs and pay for time with the strippers.

Pay for their time? Yes, pay. Pay for the thirty minutes they otherwise would have spent doing lap dances. Using that time, Heather now taught the girls that God loved and cared for them and was willing to forgive them.

Eventually Heather started a ministry called J. C.'s Girls, which she first operated in southern California and then relocated to Las Vegas. She and her partners go into strip joints and talk to the women who work there. They don't cram religion down their throats, and they don't preach to them. They just talk to them as ones who have been there. They build friendships with them. Then, when the women are ready for change, they are there to help them.

Heather says, "We go in, and whether they ever become a Christian or not, that's not the number one thing. We are there to love them and walk with them. We would love to share Jesus with them if they are open to that in their lives. It's an awesome thing."

She has become a priest to people who desperately need one.

We see the term *priest* first applied to God's people in the book of Exodus. The Jews had just been delivered by God. They had been slaves under Egyptian control for four hundred years, and then God set them free. And when God called them out of Egypt and brought them through the Red Sea, He made a remarkable statement, calling them a "kingdom of priests."[1]

To be a priest was an important position in the culture of that day. Calling a ragged group of former slaves "priests" was close to making an unbelievable declaration. I can imagine them thinking, *Who? Us? Priests? You've got to be kidding!*

But priests they were.

And the Bible says that each of us is a priest as a Christian.

You may hear that and react exactly as the Israelites did. *Who? Me? A priest?* But that is who God says you are—so who are you to argue?

John wrote in Revelation about Jesus and what He has done for us. He noted, "He has made us a *Kingdom of priests* for God his Father."[2] Whether you work at a hotel, manage a bookstore, stock shelves at a supermarket, lead a law firm, manage a medical practice, sell pharmaceuticals, or whatever, the same thing is true—if you're a Christ follower, then you're a priest.

As you discover this, everyday things take on new meaning. A simple task at work is infused with purpose because you are representing God in all you do. A conversation with a co-worker takes on greater depth because you understand your role in helping to reconcile others to God.

> You may react exactly as the Israelites did. *Who? Me? A priest?* But that is who God says you are—so who are you to argue?

Though the Israelites as a whole were called a "kingdom of priests" in the Old Testament, the specific role of a priest became limited to those who oversaw the ritual functions of worshiping God at the temple. They would offer sacrifices and intercede for the people in prayer. They would ensure that the temple property was maintained and that people could worship and experience God.

In the New Testament we see a shift, as Jesus emerges as the new High Priest who made the ultimate reconciliation between God and people at the cross. He is the mediator; we do not need to go through anyone but Jesus to get to God. Some have misinterpreted this though, as Eugene Peterson notes:

> One of the severely crippling misunderstandings of the Reformation assertion of "the priesthood of all believers" is to assume (or worse, insist) that each of us can function as our own priest—"I don't need a priest, thank you, I can do quite well on my own, me and Jesus." But that is certainly not what Martin Luther intended when he included the priesthood of all believers as a fundamental tenet for reforming the church. He meant that we are all priests, not for ourselves, but for one another. "I need you for my priest, and while we are at it, I'm available to you as your priest."[3]

As priests, we are responsible to each other and to our culture to encourage, to challenge, to walk alongside one another on this journey with Jesus. God wants to use you to make an impact for Him each day by serving as a reconciler, as a go-between for other people and Himself.

Though Jesus bridges the gap between God and people, He commissions you to lead people to God and help them find reconciliation.

When I think of this, my first reaction is to feel unworthy. The images of the deeds I've done and the words I've said make for a pretty squalid rerun. But when, at the prompting of God, I reach out and intentionally help others as a priest, I get an amazing benefit back. I feel stronger, more empowered, renewed. I live with eyes wide open.

You don't have to go to strip clubs like Heather to live as a priest. You don't even have to walk across the street. You can start right in your own home, with your own family and friends.

My friend Jane prayed every day for nineteen years that her husband would become a follower of Christ. Week in and week out, she lived with an awareness of her influence but was careful not to push. Finally he reached out to God, believed, and was baptized. He says it never would have happened if his wife had not prayed and modeled and shown love to him all those years.

As a pastor, I struggle with being a priest in my own home. When I get home after a long day of work, I just want to unplug from it all. I'm worn out and spent. But spiritual leadership for me doesn't stop at work. I'm trying to teach and lead my kids as well. We laugh and play, but I'm becoming more aware of teachable moments in everyday life to talk to them about faith and God.

Paul said in Romans, "I plead with you to give your bodies to God because of all he has done for you. Let them be a living and holy sacrifice—the kind he will find acceptable. This is truly the way to worship him."[4] Here he was echoing language used by Old Testament priests who would give sacrifices on the altar. He was saying to come and surrender your body to God. Place yourself before God as a priest placed the offering before Him.

This was a radical statement when it was written. The Jews were still offering sacrifices at the temple in Jerusalem twice daily. The term translated *worship* corresponds to a Hebrew term that refers to the technical act of worship at the temple. The implication is that we

offer ourselves as a living sacrifice as our only logical "temple worship" in light of all God has done for us in Jesus.[5]

Just as a priest in Old Testament days would offer a dead sacrifice
on the altar, so you can offer a living sacrifice of your life to God. Say
to God, "These hands are Yours; these feet are Yours; this life is Yours.
I'm not perfect, but I give myself to You." Offer yourself up to God,
and live in the surprise and spontaneity of your new identity.

Heather Veitch had offered her body in a lot of abusive ways, but
everything changed when she offered
her body to God. Her ministry took off,
and she helped many people. But when
her work with adult dancers first started
out in Southern California, do you
know who gave her the most criticism?
Christians. Christians are the ones who
have sent her hate mail and threatened
to kill her. What is *that*?

> Just as a priest in Old Testament days would offer a dead sacrifice on the altar, so you can offer a living sacrifice of your life to God.

Somehow these Christians missed the part about being priests to
a broken and hurting world.

They probably would have missed Amber too.

For several years Amber was an exotic dancer and a high-end
prostitute. She would go through the motions, acting it out with her
clients and degrading herself. Inside she was stone-cold dead. She
hated her life, and she hated God for letting her wind up in the position where she found herself.

Then a friend brought her to the most alien place imaginable—church. She felt safe enough to come to church at that time because her pimp happened to be on the run from the law. And soon Jesus reached through her rock-hard shell and stirred life in her soul.

Amber was put in touch with Heather, whose J. C.'s Girls ministry has helped her. Today Amber has left the sex business and is a chauffeur. Imagine that. She has come from a place where she was angry at God, cussing Him out, and now she's praising Him. All because someone chose to help reconcile people to God and live out her role as a priest. I can't think of anything more beautiful than that.

When Heather's work with adult dancers first started out, do you know who gave her the most criticism? Christians. Christians are the ones who have sent her hate mail and threatened to kill her.

Chapter 11

SLAVES AND SERVANTS

We've talked about how the new identity for each follower of Christ includes being a saint and a priest, a chosen child of God. This is the real me, the one God created and empowers to reach my full potential for Him. Seeing and living with eyes wide open also means embracing my identity as a servant.

One Friday, my day off, I was looking forward to relaxing around the house. When the day warmed up enough, I planned to go outside to my hammock. There I would watch the clouds go by, read a few pages of a great book, sleep a little, and watch some more clouds. The day would be beautiful. It was all mapped out in my mind.

But before I could even get started on my plan, I learned that my wife, Lori, also had some ideas about the day. She said we had shopping to do and errands to run and all sorts of domestic stuff to accomplish.

I nodded. But meanwhile I was thinking, *This is what I get on my day off—shopping?*

We climbed into the car, and I was not in a good place. Our first stop was Wal-Mart, and I was thinking, *The faster we get out of*

Wal-Mart, the faster we get to the mall and the faster I get to hammock time.

Walking into Wal-Mart, my kids noticed little carts they could ride in that play the Barney song. So I loaded them into a cart and began to push it, but it didn't move. The cart required a one-dollar bill, which none of us had.

My kids weren't letting this go, so I walked the entire Wal-Mart for at least twenty minutes and couldn't find an ATM. (As a guy, I couldn't just ask a store clerk if they had an ATM.) Finally I gave up and bought Altoids so I could get change. As I was walking back to the carts, I saw an ATM right there.

By now I was so frustrated that my face had flushed red. I put the dollar in, and away we went to the Barney song: "I love you. You love me. We're a happy family…" I pushed the cart fifty feet when my son, Ethan, tried to climb out of it. Now he wanted to get out and run and play. I said, "Ethan, you sit your bottom down right there because I spent a dollar getting the Barney music on, and we're going to listen to the Barney song. After all, we are a *happy family!*"

It was not pretty. I even saw some people from the church at Wal-Mart and immediately turned down another aisle so they wouldn't see me flustered like this.

What was the issue? I was selfish. I was angry and frustrated because I wanted to do my thing. I wanted to rest in my hammock under the sun. Because of those selfish desires, we had conflict. In fact, we didn't even go to the mall after that. Lori gave up and said, "Let's just go home." When we got home, I didn't enjoy relaxing because I felt terrible about my attitude.

•

Too often, when I look in the mirror, selfishness stares back. But the Bible says my identity is found in something else, something bigger and greater and more beautiful.

Early on, the term *servant* formed the core of the Jews' and Christians' self-understanding. Go back to the Red Sea salvation that set Israel free from Egyptian bondage. In the minds of the Hebrews, that miracle did not make them free agents who could now live it up in the desert. It made them servants of the Master who had just freed them from bondage.

"The people of Israel belong to me," God said at that juncture in history. "They are my servants, whom I brought out of the land of Egypt. I am the LORD your God."[1] The Hebrews were free from Egyptian bondage, but they were not free from God.

Being a servant is a high and honored position in the Bible. Jesus was the greatest servant of all, who challenged us to remember that the last will be first. When you look in the mirror, remind yourself that you are not a slave to sin but a servant to freedom.

Servants are free from the constant one-upping mentality that drives so many in our culture. They are free from the relentless need for attention, for affirmation, for the spotlight. They are free from so many games that go on in the name of success. They aren't worried about spreading their fame but instead go about spreading the fame of God. Their joy is found in Him, and their recognition comes from serving Him.

Sometimes I fall prey to a false idealism where I think I have to do something *huge* to be a real servant. I've gone on mission trips around the world to serve others. I've worked in underground churches in Belarus and in the slums of Ecuador and in one of the poorest areas of the Dominican Republic called "the hole." These were challenging experiences, but each time I came back motivated to stop looking *elsewhere* to be a servant and start serving in little ways now. The little things are the big things.

I've started to think about being a servant with much less idealistic questions: "God, how do You want me to serve my kids, my spouse, or my friend? How can I be a servant at work today? At the grocery store? Driving in traffic?"

I will never forget my friend Mike telling me what got him through some tough times growing up in Southern California. Every school day when he was growing up, his dad would take a yellow sticky note and write a simple encouragement and slip it in Mike's lunch. He'd say, "Son, I love you." "You are doing great, kid." "I'm so proud of you."

Mike said, "My dad will never know that there were moments, especially in the teenage years, when I was barely hanging on. What I was hanging on to were those little yellow notes that reminded me I could pull through this. Somebody believed in me and loved me."

What was his dad doing? He was being a servant. Do you know what Mike does now? He writes little encouraging notes to his kids.

This has helped me simplify my approach to helping others. You change the world one act of kindness at a time.

Here's a bit of reality. When we become believers, many of us think, *Well, yeah, I have certain gifts and abilities.* But then we begin to stall. We start thinking like this: *You know, I don't have my life all together yet. I still have bad habits. I still have issues. If the people at church knew what they were, they just wouldn't believe how I keep messing up. I need a little time because right now God isn't ready to use me.*

Or we think, *After I get my life together, once I get perfect, then God will use me.* Good luck with that!

That's not the way God works. Look through the Bible—God uses imperfect, broken, hurting people everywhere. Being broken and hurting and imperfect is the human condition. It's what being human means in a fallen world. Who else is God going to use?

I love this little piece that someone wrote years ago. It goes through many of the famous Bible characters. You may not know who these people are or what they've done, but know that God used them to turn the world upside down.

> You change the world one act of kindness at a time.

Moses stuttered. David's armor didn't fit. John Mark was rejected by Paul. Hosea's wife was a prostitute—what must his friends have thought? Amos's only training was in the school of fig tree pruning. Solomon was too rich. Abraham was too old. David was too young. Timothy had ulcers. Peter was afraid of death. And Lazarus was dead.

John was self-righteous. Naomi was a widow. Paul was a murderer—and so was Moses (two people who transformed the world, yet could have been on death row). Jonah ran from God. Miriam was a gossip. Gideon and Thomas both were doubters. Jeremiah was depressed and suicidal. Elijah was burned out. John the Baptist was a loudmouth. Martha was a worrywart. Mary was lazy. And Samson had long hair. (Yes, God can use people with long hair!)

But here's the thing. God doesn't look at our financial gain or loss. That's not what it's about with him. He's not prejudiced or partial. He's not judging or begrudging or sassy or brassy. He's not deaf to our cry or blind to our need. As much as we try to work for them, God's gifts are free.[2]

We didn't earn these gifts, and we don't deserve them. God uses imperfect people. In your brokenness, in your messed-up situation, He can use you to impact other people.

At one point, Paul wrote of a time when he had a struggle or weakness in his life. He went to God again and again, asking Him to take it away. Some commentators have said it may have been malaria or some other crippling or debilitating condition. Others speculate it was a temptation he constantly struggled with. Either way, God responded, "My grace is all you need. My power works best in weakness."

We may think we need physical heal-ing or empowerment for our struggles, and sometimes we do. But other times what we really need is to acknowledge the truth of grace. To realize that God provides comfort and grace *in proportion to the need*. "So now I am glad to boast about my weaknesses," Paul finally was able to say, "so that the power of Christ can work through me."[3]

> The main thing is not how talented we are or how good we are or how we feel about ourselves. The main thing is that we lever-age our gifts for God's glory, serving in what-ever way we can.

Do you know the greatest lesson I've learned over the years about serving God with our gifts? It's that the gifts are not about us. They are about God. The main thing is not how talented we are or how good we are or how we feel about ourselves. The main thing is that we leverage those gifts for God's glory, serving in whatever way we can.

I've been through seasons when I was bored with my faith. It was sort of like I was saying—*yawn*—"Yeah, I'm a Christian. I'm in." Can you relate? During those times, my boredom emerged because I wasn't using the gifts God had given me to make a difference in other people's lives. Apathy starts with self-comfort. Once I got out there and started doing something, I suddenly began to see God working again. The adventure of life and faith became real again.

Like the guy who wrote me a note:

My life used to be about one thing—me. I was a self-serving guy who had neither purpose nor passion. I was leading a miserable life, throwing away time and money on beer and cheap thrills. Then one day I walked into a church and heard the message of Christ: *Give your life away to others, and you will find your life.* I didn't have much to give up, so I decided to give it a shot.

That's when my life started to change and Christ became more real to me. I started serving teenagers and found a purpose—a reason for my existence.

It was twenty-one years ago that I wandered into that church. Today my life is richer than I ever believed it could be. Serving others made the difference. It was one of the best decisions I ever made.

He learned to see himself as a servant. He's now living the adventure of his new identity.

Part 3

WIDE OPEN TO CHANGE

Chapter 12

THE TROUBLE
WITH U-HAUL

Remember the old fun-house mirrors at the carnival that would reflect those freakishly distorted images of yourself? You'd get up close and your face would appear three times as wide as it really was. You'd seem to be eight feet tall with huge feet, a pencil-thin body, and a distorted head that ran all the way up to the ceiling.

Sometimes we see God and ourselves in a fun-house mirror. Our distorted images wreak havoc in our lives and greatly limit our possibilities. We've been learning how to correct these distorted images, how living with eyes wide open involves seeing differently. We've explored the importance of seeing God clearly and understanding His perspective. This reorients our view of just about everything else in our lives. Once I surrender my view of myself and embrace God's view of me, I am free to live the real me. I'm free to become the person God created me to be.

We've also learned about our new identity as God changes us positionally to be a saint, priest, and servant. Someone defined not by our struggles but by His grace and love.

The adventure is not just seeing with less distortion but living with less distortion. God didn't give us a new identity so that we could remain the same. He desires for us to grow and be transformed into a person more in line with that identity.

People today are obsessed with the idea of changing themselves. Every year Americans spend billions of dollars trying to transform their bodies. Clothing, cosmetics, weight loss, personal trainers, and makeover surgery—all to look better and sexier. American men and women, including teenagers, spent roughly $15 billion for a hundred kinds of nips and tucks last year.[1] Sometimes the surgeries go well, but not always.

Consider Priscilla Presley, Elvis's widow and a *Dancing with the Stars* celebrity, who had a less-than-successful facial surgery. Pictures of the "new" and not-as-becoming Priscilla are, sadly enough, all over the Internet. It's as if people can't get enough of her personal misfortune.

Now the facelift-that-flunks doesn't just happen to women. Gary Busey, a movie star now in his midsixties, had some work done recently. And looking at his picture, you probably find yourself thinking, *Will the real Gary Busey please stand up?*

We spend hundreds of billions of dollars to transform our bodies. Sure, the outside work can be done quickly. You schedule an appointment, wreck your checkbook, get the surgery, and unless you're one of the unfortunate ones whose face work goes south, you're good. Most of the lines are gone from your face, and you transform your body with a ninety-day workout program. But all the while, real transforming needs to be done on the inside, which can take years, even decades. It is a lifelong process of change where you "put on your new nature" and are "renewed as you learn to know your Creator and become like him."[2]

This change process is a lifelong journey filled with ups and downs. It requires us to take relational risks and drop our masks with God and others. It calls out our secrets and presses us to stop lying to ourselves. It digs into our thought patterns and challenges us to depend more on God's Spirit. And this process of change is impossible without others around us encouraging and motivating us. But it is also where the joy is. As we become more like Christ, we are filled with characteristics we all want—things like love, joy, peace, patience, and kindness. We become more of the real person God desires.

> I feared that becoming a believer would mean that I would no longer be a unique person but an imitation—think like all other Christians, dress like them, wear my hair like them, listen to the same music. What I discovered was the opposite. As I embrace God's view of me, I become more fully my own self.

Before I became a Christian, I feared that becoming a believer would mean I'd lose my individuality. That I would no longer be a unique person but an imitation—think like all other Christians, dress like them, wear my hair like them, listen to the same music. What I discovered was the opposite. As I embrace God's view of me, I become more fully my own self, the real person He designed me to be.

Too many times we miss this fact because we go to church and think, *I raised my hand during that prayer. I was baptized. So I'm covered—I'm saved.* Sometimes we think we're done, but really it's only the beginning. God now wants to start shaping us into the people He desires for us to be. First we see God and ourselves differently; then we begin to live it out differently.

Is it possible to be a Christian and be a miserable, life-draining, and negative person? I've known a few. These people have accepted Christ and have asked Him into their hearts. And that's great. But they're still in their highchairs, banging their spoons for attention.

Yes, He has saved us. But now He wants to bring a change from the inside out—He wants to do a great work in our lives if we will only let Him. But there is no quick fix.

> You get to the new destination, the new house, the new relationship, and you get everything all set up. But the problem is still *you.*

I'm writing this from Las Vegas, and thousands of people move here each year to start over. *It's going to be a new day,* they think. *Let's pull up all our stakes and move to Vegas.* Or they jump into a new relationship. *Hey, now I've got a fresh start. With this person, I'm going to be okay.* But there's a maxim in recovery: "Wherever you go, there you are."

You can't run away from the stuff inside. You bring it with you. It's the psychological equivalent of loading up a U-Haul and moving on. Do you know why they call it a U-Haul? Because it's *you* hauling it. You get to the new destination, the new house, the new relationship, and you get everything all set up. But the problem is still *you.*

It's just a matter of time before the same cycle starts again. Unless you let God into the deeper recesses of your life and let Him do the work He wants to do.

When Lori and I bought a new master bed for the Wilhite house, we faced what I call "The Curse of New Furniture"—all the old furniture immediately looked bad.

Our new bed frame and headboard were made from a very dark wood, but our dresser set was light. Now, this dresser set was handed down through Lori's great-grandmother to her grandma and then to us. So we decided to "restore" the family heirloom dressers. We carried both dressers down the stairs of our house and into the garage to stain them dark brown to match the bed frame.

I went to the home-improvement store and told the in-store "expert" about the bedroom pieces I wanted to restore.

"No problem," he said. "You can do a shortcut to restoration. All you have to do is take steel wool and rub it on the wood. Then take this primer I'm going to give you and put it on. And then apply the stain. You won't have to sand it down or anything—you can do it all in one night, and it will look beautiful."

Back home, I steel-wooled both dressers, primed them, and stained them. *Man, is this easy,* I thought. I left them in the garage to dry overnight.

Twenty-four hours later I walked into our garage and saw that the dressers were dripping onto the newspapers I'd put beneath them. They were still wet and gooey.

It turned out that the guy at the hardware store had given me a can of *water*-based primer and a can of *oil*-based stain. (That's why

I didn't mention the name of the home-improvement store to you. Think orange.)

Now I had to wipe the whole thing down and get all the goo cleared off. I had to sand the wood down and do it right. This took weeks. I was in my garage all hours of the night. Finally we got the pieces down to their original condition, and *then* we stained and restored them.

They look amazing.

That sanding and goo-removal process made me think about the work of God in our lives. Too often in our spiritual lives we would love a shortcut. Just rub some steel wool over the surface of our lives, put on a primer and a stain, and we'll be ready to go.

But real restoration isn't a one-night deal. It's a lifelong process, painful at times, challenging at others. It means that we let Jesus, the master carpenter, get beneath the veneer of our hearts and do the long-term spiritual work He wants to do.

> Real restoration isn't a one-night deal. It's a lifelong process, painful at times, challenging at others.

Spiritual growth and spiritual becoming aren't a simple linear process that moves from point A to point B. It's better to see spiritual growth more like a spiral that's gradually moving toward a destination of becoming like Jesus. You may head this way for a while and you may head that way, but you're still moving toward the destination. You are becoming the person God already says you are.

Henry Cloud has noted that growth is a process that looks like this:

Grace + Truth + Time = Growth[3]

All of these elements must be working together.

Grace is recognizing that we are accepted and understanding that God is for us. Grace is all about the radical mercy of God in our lives. But grace in a vacuum is not enough without truth—facing the truth about ourselves and the truth of who God says we are.

If you only have grace, you'll be forgiven, but you won't be challenged by the truth to become the person God desires. You'll be stuck in a rut. So truth must be there as well. Yet if you only have truth, without grace, you'll wallow in guilt and condemnation.

And all of this takes significant time. The change doesn't happen overnight. If we don't recognize this fact, we'll be discouraged when we fail, and the same patterns will continue to show themselves.

God wants you to experience the adventure of not only *seeing* but also *living* the real you, the one He created you to be. Don't rush it. And don't get discouraged if it's taking longer than you expected. Stick with the change process, and watch God form you into the work of art He has in mind.

Chapter 13

DROP THE MASK

Y ou may have had the misfortune of watching the movie *Mean Girls*. I'm still trying to figure out how this happened to me. It's not so much a movie as a vehicle by which Lindsay Lohan became even more "Lindsay Lohan" for the paparazzi.

The flick is about high school kids and all the backbiting cliques they fall into. At one point, the movie shows a map of the school's "central nervous system"—the cafeteria. The camera then scans around the cafeteria to reveal all the different groups, including the too-cool kids, the way-smart kids, the jocks, the freaks, the geeks, and then the teenage royalty. This last is a superficial group known in the movie as the Plastics.

The Plastics are three rich girls who use gossip, power games, and fake popularity to rule their kingdom. For them, it's all about fitting in with each other so that they can survive and succeed in the world of high school.

Mean Girls does a pretty good job of showing how the desire to fit in persuades people to put on masks.

We wear masks when we pretend to be something or someone we're not or when we hide our true feelings. For some it's easier to fit in by submerging their feelings rather than dealing with them straight on. The scary thing is that we can play a role so often that we lose contact with who's really behind the mask.

Masks, of course, have been around from the beginning of time. Without masks there would have been no ancient theater, no Halloween, and no Mardi Gras. There's something about masks that conjures up mystery and intrigue.

> We wear masks when we pretend to be something or someone we're not or when we hide our true feelings. The scary thing is that we can play a role so often that we lose contact with who's really behind the mask.

One of the most popular acts in recent history is the Blue Man Group, a trio of mute performers who wear blue greasepaint, latex bald caps that make them appear earless, and black clothing.

What makes them so intriguing?

For one thing, each blue man is totally silent, and his face is expressionless. A blue man never communicates with words. Only by eye contact and discreet, simple gestures does a blue man move you. But move you he does, as demonstrated by the group's popularity.

Do you think it's possible that so many people connect with the Blue Man Group because so many of us hide behind masks ourselves? Because we can't let our true selves become known? Because we, too, are playacting and are forced to conform? Because we are afraid that if we let our real feelings be known, people might laugh at us or pigeonhole us or decide that we don't fit in?

Of course, it could also be because they play a killer drum set and release toilet paper all over the audience. But work with me here.

Wherever we go, people are wearing masks.

For instance, there's always someone who wears the "funny guy" mask. He's the life of the party and he's always smiling, even when he doesn't want to smile. Then there's the "tough guy" or "tough girl" mask. Nothing ever gets to the tough ones. They're in your office. They work the checkout lines. They're at the club. They pass out the popcorn at the Cineplex. Everything's cool, everything's okay. The mask goes on even when things aren't okay.

There's even a church mask.

"Hey, good to see you. How's it going today?"

"Doin' just fine, thanks." And inside, that person is yearning to tell someone that his life is in disarray—only church isn't the place to do that. People wouldn't take the time to truly listen anyway, and what's the use of imposing?

"Just fine, thanks."

It goes on like this over and over again, as we live in a world of unreality.

> Our masks form one of the greatest barriers between us and God, between us and others. This is why God desires that we be true and consistent down to the core.

But why do we want to live there—in that fake world? Maybe we're afraid that if we lower our mask, others won't like what they see. Or we're afraid that we wouldn't get what we want. Or we're afraid that after taking the risk to be real, no one would care anyway.

Our masks form one of the greatest barriers between us and God, between us and others. This is why God desires that we be true and consistent down to the core. It's sad to say, but religious people have been missing this transformation since time immemorial.

Back in Jesus' time, there was a group of religious teachers called the Pharisees. They were the popular religious leaders of the Jewish middle class, and they resisted being shaped from the inside out. They went to the temple, learned their Bibles by rote, and in their own way sought to obey what God had laid out. But in many ways they were only playing the game, going through the motions without any real internal change taking place. Sound familiar?

Here's what Jesus said to them: "Woe to you, teachers of the law and Pharisees, you hypocrites! You clean the outside of the cup and dish, but inside they are full of greed and self-indulgence. Blind Pharisee! First clean the inside of the cup and dish, and then the outside also will be clean."[1]

Have you ever been at a nice restaurant and had food brought out in an elaborate way, only to find something disgusting in your food? A hair, for instance. There's nothing like pulling a long blond hair out of your pasta—when you have short brown hair. One friend of mine found a cockroach in her salad. Another found a piece of glass on her plate.

The term Jesus used for "dish" represented a fine plate on which food would be served. The dish was beautiful, like your best china, but the food on the dish in Jesus' story would give you food poisoning.

He was saying that the religious leaders of the day looked great on the outside—their dishes were like spectacular china—but inside they were full of deceit, catering to their own personal whims and desires. Lots of glass, hair, and worse in those dishes. The term Jesus used for "greed" literally implies robbery, plundering, or even extortion. They played the part externally but were robbing people for their own pleasure.

Maybe we're not exactly like the Pharisees, but this game of being one person in public and another in private is one we all play to some extent or another. It is prompted by the human condition and aided and abetted by the evil one, who keeps whispering in our ear, "No one's interested in your baggage—they have enough problems of their own."

But we owe it to ourselves to take the chance to come clean. To make it a point to talk to *someone*. Someone who will listen. Someone who's been broken himself or herself. Someone who won't blow you off for lowering the mask. There are people out there who will listen if you ask for a moment in private and decide to get real.

A while back, I went through a season of struggle with extreme frustration and anger. I'd be impatient with my wife, harsh with my kids, and mad at the Dallas Cowboys football team.

For a long time I blamed my attitude on the fact that I was too busy, too stressed, overwhelmed. My excuses seemed justified, and I kept rationalizing the junk stewing inside.

One night my wife, Lori, was at the grocery store during our kids' bedtime, so I had to put Emma and Ethan to bed. I was flying out for a big meeting the next morning, and I was in a rush, still needing to finish the laundry and pack. Three different times my five-year-old daughter, Emma, climbed out of bed. Three different times I went upstairs and had to nag her to go to sleep. I grew more and more frustrated with the situation. *Where's Lori? Why did she leave me in charge of the kids, knowing I have so much to do tonight?*

Then, while downstairs in the laundry room, I heard Emma's little feet hit the floor as she crawled out of bed for the fourth time. I went postal, psycho, and ballistic all at once. (Gifted and talented, wouldn't you say?)

I slammed my fist into the Sheetrock of the Wilhite laundry room, leaving a hole in the wall.

As I stared at the hole, I thought, *Great! That's embarrassing. Real mature, Jud.*

Then a far scarier thought scrolled through my mind: *Is this what you are becoming?*

That thought had the effect of sobering me up and calming me down. I went upstairs and tucked my daughter into bed. Then I returned to the laundry room, gazed at my handiwork, and thought, *Lori will never see it. And if she does, I'll tell her I bumped into the wall with the broom handle.* Totally lame, of course, but I was a desperate man.

Soon after this event, Lori walked into the laundry room and said, "Jud, why is there a hole in the wall?"

Everything in me wanted to lie. I looked Lori in the eye and said, "Because your husband…uh…sort of…like…hit the wall." She raised her eyebrows.

"Promise me you won't tell anyone I hit the wall?" This gave an extra lift to Lori's eyebrows.

Some time later I was preparing to give a weekend message on temptation. Just before I walked out to speak, I sensed God lay on my heart that I needed to come clean about the hole in the wall. I wrestled with Him internally for a few moments and then surrendered to the idea.

> The people who really count in your life don't want you with a mask on. They want you— the *real* you.

As I talked about the experience with our church, I felt walls come down all over the room. All weekend, people came up to me who'd had the same problem or acted out in similar ways. One person said, "Okay, Jud, if you're going to be honest and genuine with no games, I will be as well."

Here's the thing: The people who really count in your life don't want you with a mask on. They want you—the *real* you. You don't have to hide behind anything. Just be *you*. And know that when you lower the mask so a friend can see the real you, you move closer to the God who has seen and known the real you all along.

Chapter 14

POST YOUR SECRET

We use masks because we don't like who we really *are*. We keep secrets because we don't like what we've really *done* or what has really *happened to us*. These are closely related, yet change depends on both being real about who you are and being truthful about what you have done and experienced. Dropping masks requires authenticity; facing secrets requires confession.

Confession is the idea behind PostSecret. It began as a simple art project where you create your own four-by-six-inch postcard out of any mailable material, write a secret on it, and mail it in to Post-Secret headquarters. The secret could be anything—a hope, a fear, a feeling, a humiliation—as long as you hadn't told anyone else about it.

The response to PostSecret has been overwhelming. People all over the world have seized upon this outlet to anonymously confess their secrets. After all, even writing a secret to a stranger can bring some healing.

Some of the postcards are powerful; some are offensive or even perverse. But they all offer a glimpse into the human soul:

- "I haven't spoken to my dad in 10 years…and it kills me every day."
- "I feel guilty all the time."
- "I miss feeling close to God."
- "Sometimes I want to run away from home. (I'm 38 and married with a child.)"
- "I give decaf to customers who are rude to me!" (This was from a Starbucks employee. Come to think of it, I don't get the kick out of Starbucks I once did. Hmm.)
- "I am a peaceful person who happens to be filled with violent rage."
- "He's been in prison for two years because of what I did."[1]

We carry around the scars of our past in deep and profound ways. We often wear masks in the first place because we carry secrets that corrode our sense of worth. A secret is about a formative event or experience or a consistent failing. What we don't realize is that our secrets grow in destructive power the longer we keep them in the dark. They tend to isolate and sometimes drive us away from others and from God. Researchers have only recently begun to investigate how secrecy and nondisclosure can influence people's physical and mental health. But studies already show that those who keep lots of secrets about their personal life have more physical and emotional issues.

> Our secrets grow in destructive power the longer we keep them in the dark.

Keeping harmful secrets takes effort. It requires the brain and the heart to work harder. Obsessive thoughts often develop around a secret. It just takes over, doesn't it? Before we know it, our secrets from the past rob us of our present and our future.

Keeping a secret doesn't mean you're an evil person. It doesn't mean you're not loved by God. It simply means you're ashamed of what you're doing or of what has taken control of you. And you fear what people might think if you ever let it out. But experiencing grace and truth with people and with God can set you free.

I have a friend named Susan who has a secret. Susan is a flight attendant, and one day a fellow attendant told her she loved playing the slots in Las Vegas. She almost invariably won more than she lost. Susan was intrigued. So a short while later she went to a casino and started playing the penny and nickel machines. She wagered fifteen dollars and came home with a hundred.

Susan was married to an airline pilot who was away from home much of the time. Meanwhile, her own schedule of flights was being reduced, and she spent most of what had become a series of lonely days at the slots. She couldn't get enough of the rush they provided. She once won four thousand dollars in an afternoon, and in the beginning she often made more money in a few hours than she could make in the air on a three-day trip.

> Keeping a secret doesn't mean you're an evil person. It simply means you're ashamed of what you're doing or of what has taken control of you. And you fear what people might think if you ever let it out.

"It was like Monopoly money to me," she says. And for a month or two she always seemed to be landing on Boardwalk or Park Place. She kept her secret from her husband.

How do you know when something that started innocently is becoming dangerous? How do you know when something is getting a grip on your life? You start keeping it a secret. You start hiding it. That's what happened with Susan.

Even though she had been a Christian for many years, Susan allowed her secret to grow and develop. She could sit in front of the slots for ten hours and zone out the world. But after a number of months, her luck began to change. First she was no longer winning as much, then she was barely breaking even, and eventually she was getting deeper and deeper in the hole.

By this time she had quit praying and stopped attending church. She kept the gambling from her husband when he was home but spent every day at the casino when he was away. "You get real defiant on the outside and have complete denial on the inside," she says. "You say to yourself, 'I can control this or stop it if I want to.'"

But she couldn't stop it. And "on the inside," she says, "I just hated myself."

The slots were an antidote for her loneliness when her husband was away. The sensation made her blood flow. She would go home dehydrated because she didn't drink anything at the slots and would never take a break to get something to eat.

Susan played a shell game with her credit cards, taking money from one to pay off the other. Eventually she ran up ninety thousand dollars in debt from the slots and was harboring a secret that was destroying her life.

Finally, inevitably, her husband, Max, found out. There was a huge argument; he was filled with anger and disbelief. He felt that all he had worked for was being flushed away. After many relapses on Susan's part, he refused to stand by and watch everything they had built be destroyed. He still loved her, but he threatened to leave if she didn't get help.

"Every time we fought over it, every time he found out, I would go back and slip up again," Susan says. "I promised him I don't know how many times that I was going to quit. And every time I didn't, it was like I'd taken a knife and driven it into his heart."

After threatening to leave her repeatedly, Max finally gave her a note: "If you ever steal from me again, I will turn you in. I will not enable you any more.... If you ever steal from me again, I will immediately start divorce proceedings."

Then, from out of nowhere, Susan's son reminded her that she was the reason he had become a Christian the previous year. She was his rock. Therefore, he said, she *had* to turn her life back over to God. How could his rock slip into the sea?

This was the turning point. That very night she got down on her knees and prayed. She asked desperately for God's help, and the recovery process began.

She reached out to others and leaned on friends and her church. She stopped doing this part of her life alone.

As Susan got honest with God and trusted friends about her secret, she found freedom. At this writing, she hasn't gambled in six months. "I've got a lot of work to do, a lot of debt to pay off, and a lot of damage to repair," Susan says. "I can see now that God was there waiting to bring me out of it at any time. But I wouldn't ask Him and wouldn't invite Him in. I've done that now. I'm right where I think God wants me to be."

Susan is finding healing and forgiveness. Her secret is no longer destroying her. There *is* help, and God is still there in the darkest night.

You might be surprised to know that the apostle Paul also had something of a secret—something he had to overcome. The letter of Romans recounts his spiritual struggle. Have you ever fought lust or despair or depression or estrangement so severe that you thought death might actually be better? We have no way of knowing for sure, but those demons may have been the personal secrets Paul was writing about in Romans 7.

"I've tried everything and nothing helps," he said at one point. "I'm at the end of my rope. Is there no one who can do anything for me? Isn't that the real question?"[2]

Paul declared, "What a wretched man I am! Who will rescue me from this body of death?"[3]

This term "body of death" was graphic and showed the extent of his struggle. Near Tarsus, Paul's birthplace, an ancient tribe dealt harshly with murderers. A convicted murderer would be strapped to the dead body of the slain. He would remain strapped there until the decay of the corpse infected him and killed him. Maybe this is what Paul was referring to when he spoke of his "body of death."[4]

Paul said, in essence, "I just can't escape from myself and this sin nature within me. It is bound to me," just like the rotting corpse was tied to the doomed victim.

Then, in a burst of sunlight, he said the following, as if overcoming this living death: "The answer, thank God, is that Jesus Christ can and does. He acted to set things right in this life of contradictions where I want to serve God with all my heart and mind, but am pulled by the influence of sin to do something totally different."[5]

Yes, like Paul, we have secrets and struggles. We know what goes on in our minds and hearts when we are alone. How can we get free from it? The answer is that Jesus Christ can and does rescue us. The means of overcoming our weaknesses in life is not willpower or self-help but the living power of Christ. That power is available when we get honest about our secrets with God and others.

> The confession of our sins can be so healthy. It's a sign of a heart that is ready for change and healing.

This is why the confession of our sins can be so healthy. It's a sign of a heart that is ready for change and healing.

After we confess to God, it's crucial to confess to others, as advised in the Bible: "Confess your sins to each other and pray for each other so that you may be healed."[6] Notice the condition for healing: *confession*. We'd rather camouflage our sins than confess them. Still, it's liberating to confess our sins, not just to God but to each other.

Does that mean you should confess to the whole world? Definitely not. Scripture says to confess our sins, not broadcast them.

There's a principle called "the circle of confession," which teaches that we should confess only as widely as our sin involves other people. If I've got a private sin, just between me and God, then I ought to confess it just to God. If it's a personal sin, between me and you, then I need to come to you as well as to God.

Confession looses the hold of sin and releases the power of God. To live with eyes wide open is to face our secrets and bring them into the light. In the process, we become fully and completely alive.

Chapter 15

MIND
YOUR OWN BUSINESS

Change doesn't break through in our lives until we get real, drop our masks, and face our secrets. But the change won't last until we take control of our thought life and replace destructive thoughts with biblical ones.

I don't know how they counted this up or what kind of brain transmitters they had to install, but neuroscientists say that on average a person thinks about fifty thousand thoughts a day.[1] Research demonstrates that every thought sends electrical and chemical signals throughout your brain, ultimately affecting each cell in your body. This may send a shudder through you, but thoughts can influence your heart rate, your sleeping patterns, your digestion, and even your blood's chemical makeup. And according to some researchers, approximately 90 percent of the thoughts we have are repeats from yesterday or the day before.[2]

This is why the Bible teaches that our thoughts are key to changing. "Let God transform you into a new person by changing the way you think."[3] The biblical word translated as "transformed" is a term from which we get the word *metamorphosis*. Morphing starts in the mind, with a different way of thinking—with a different way of seeing, you might say.

To morph tomorrow, we must actively take control of our thoughts today. We can't be passive or lazy about them.

I recently read *The 4:8 Principle* by Tommy Newberry. The book challenged me in how I was managing my thought life and helped me to see how undisciplined I'd become.

Tommy talks of how his eight-year-old son, Ty, broke his arm on his first day of football practice. Over the next several days, Ty would fall into negative spirals of thinking about all the things he couldn't do with a broken arm. But his dad refused to let him live there. He asked Ty to write out a list of twenty-one things he *could* do with a broken arm.

> To morph tomorrow, we must actively take control of our thoughts today.

Ty sat down and started his list. "I could hike or run," he wrote. "I could play in my tree house. I could go to the movies, eat popcorn, and have M&M's. I could still do science experiments. I could do sit-ups, take a bath, and make my bed."[4] Ty went on and on. He actually got excited as he wrote out all he could do.

This is an example of how changing our perspective on a tough situation can make a significant difference. I've been working this principle into my life, being more disciplined in my thoughts about challenges, and it's bringing me more joy.

I'm learning that I fall into negative spirals without even realizing it. When my calendar gets really full, for example, sometimes I'm tempted to wallow in thoughts of how trapped I'm going to be by all I've got scheduled. But as I control my thoughts, I realize the opportunities God has given through these things. I think of the special family times we'll work in. I visualize the people I'll be able to encourage. I focus on the life-giving aspects of what's on my calendar in days ahead. This is one way I'm fighting sin and temptation in my life.

The power of our thoughts is well recognized but often misguided.

Rhonda Byrne has led a thought movement through her book *The Secret.* For months it topped the bestseller list and was featured on *Oprah,* along with a slew of other talk shows. Byrne suggests that you basically have unlimited power with your thought life and can attract health, wealth, and everything you ever wanted. This is called the *law of attraction*—you attract what you think about. *The Secret* postulates that the law of attraction is like gravity, unavoidable and always present. Do you want to be a billionaire? Then you'd better start thinking about tons of cash. If you do, the law of attraction will bring riches into your life.

In *The Secret,* God is perceived to be like a genie. In fact, if you're using the book's accompanying DVD, you'll see a genie lamp pop up on the screen and then suddenly become the Universe with a capital *U.* The Universe says to you, "Your wish is my command." Wow, that's good to know!

Whatever you want you can have because you've accepted the belief that your wish is the Universe's command. If you go to the Web site for *The Secret,* you'll see something that looks like a check.

It says, "UNIVERSAL BANK (UN)LIMITED," with a little genie lamp in the top left corner. You can fill out the check for whatever amount of money you want—millions, billions, whatever. Just don't think small.

Then the next step—you visualize it. According to *The Secret*, if you think about it long enough, money will start to show up in your life. And all this time you thought you had to go to work! No, you just think *money*, and it's supposed to flow into your life.

We are to focus our minds on things that are excellent and worthy of praise because there is power in the mind. But not just for our own selfish gain.

Do *The Secret* and the Bible teach the same things? Well, they both affirm the principle that there is power in the way you think. But beyond that, there are real, tangible, and even radical differences between the two. *The Secret* seems to imply that you are in a universe all by yourself. Whatever you want you can have. The problem is, we live in a universe with all kinds of people, and we're affected by decisions others make and things others do. Our decisions have an impact on other people as well. What if you're thinking *snow* and your neighbor is thinking *sunshine*? What about things like poverty and injustice? Are there not many hard and negative things we must think about and confront in order to make our world a better place?

The Bible emphasizes the power of our thoughts: "Fix your thoughts on what is true, and honorable, and right, and pure, and lovely, and admirable. Think about things that are excellent and worthy of praise."[5] We are to focus our minds on these things because there is power in the mind. But not just for our own selfish gain. Not just so the universe can be at our beck and call.

The Bible teaches that the world and the universe are not about us. They're about God. They're about His fame, His glory, His power and might. Understanding this, and then living in it, becomes one of the most challenging lessons we can learn, but it frees us to live with great joy and surrender in the moment.

> When I hear a voice in my head saying that I'm not worthy and God doesn't care about me, I counter that by speaking God's Word to myself.

I'm not a proponent of positive thinking in a vacuum, but of biblical thinking, which is positive, realistic, and helpful. For years I've embraced something Martyn Lloyd-Jones taught when he said we should talk to ourselves more than we listen to ourselves. He didn't mean that we should split our personalities, but that we should remind ourselves throughout the day of what the Bible says.

When I hear a voice in my head saying that I'm not worthy and God doesn't care about me, I counter that by speaking God's Word to myself. I don't walk around talking out loud to myself, but I do mentally remind myself of passages that override the negative messages that play in my mind. I remind myself that "there is now no condemnation for those who are in Christ Jesus." I repeat, "'I know the plans I have for you,' says the LORD. 'They are plans for good and not for disaster, to give you a future and a hope.'" I quote, "Perfect love expels all fear" and "If God is for us, who can ever be against us?"⁶ In doing this, I let God's Word clear my sightlines.

If becoming the real you depends so much on your thoughts, how could your life be different if you thought differently?

What if you imagined a world where you made an eternal difference in the lives of others?

What if you saw yourself as forgiven and free, a servant of God on a mission every day?

What if you saw bitterness toward someone who has hurt you turning to forgiveness?

What would happen if you opened your eyes to what you can do for God, not to what you can't?

You might well find yourself praying for the poor and the hurting rather than avoiding them. You'd probably find time to reach out to them and help them.

You'd likely find yourself becoming more of the person God desires, more of the person you desire—the real you.

Chapter 16

BE FILLED

Ever get frustrated because you think you should be growing more, learning more, or accomplishing more? I do. In those moments, I find it helps to remember that even when it feels like I'm standing still, the earth is moving, God is moving, and unseen things are happening.

This struck me powerfully as I read about Johnny Cash.[1] Cash was born into a dirt-poor family in Arkansas during the Great Depression. By the age of five, he was already working in the cotton fields with his family. He was surrounded by the church, gospel music, and the radio, beamed from across the Mississippi River from Memphis, Tennessee, some thirty-five miles away.

Johnny—or J. R., as they called him then—was a creative child, a constant dreamer, drawn to music from the very beginning. It often put him at odds with his hard-working blue-collar father.

J. R. idolized his brother Jack, and a terrible incident when he was twelve and Jack was fourteen marked him forever.

Jack was working in a sawmill one day when he slipped and was drawn onto the blade of a spinning power saw. He was sliced open from his neck to his hip in a ghastly accident. Jack hung on for a week before he died, and J. R., devastated, blamed himself for not being able to rescue him. He left home as a teenager several years later, indelibly marked by the memory.

After a hitch in the military, Johnny Cash returned to Memphis in the 1950s looking for freedom and success as a musician. He quickly found both. He met Sam Phillips of Sun Records and plunged into the life of a touring musician. He found immediate success and soon was on the road more than at home. But problems were brewing.

In his autobiography, *Cash,* he said, "My affair with pills had already begun. It quickly became all-consuming, eating me up for the next decade or so."[2]

Perhaps as a way to deal with his success and his taxing life as a performer, his strained relationships and his continual running from Jesus, he yielded to the temptation all around. He worshiped music and the various substances that sustained him. The endless cycle of alcohol and drugs, almost to the exclusion of food, was slowly proving lethal.

Cash said of his addictions, "The first and perhaps worst thing about it was that every pill I took was an attempt to regain the wonderful natural feeling of euphoria I experienced the first time. And there was not a single one, not even a single one of these, that did not tear me away from my family, my God and myself."[3]

Bit by bit, Johnny Cash destroyed the life he led. He wrecked numerous cars and was arrested for buying massive amounts of amphetamines across the Mexican border. He wound up canceling shows and whole tours. He even carelessly burned several hundred acres of the Los Padres National Forest and was sued by the state of California.

Perhaps worst of all, he completely wrecked his marriage and left his four daughters virtually fatherless.

One thing you didn't see in the 2005 movie on Cash, called *Walk the Line,* was that when he hit rock bottom through drugs, he decided to take his own life. He said, "I never wanted to see another dawn. I had wasted my life. I had drifted so far away from God and every stabilizing force in my life that I felt there was no hope for me. I knew what to do. I'd go into Nickajack Cave…and let God take me from this earth and put me wherever He puts people like me."[4]

As a child, he had explored the depths of Nickajack Cave not far from Lookout Mountain near Chattanooga, Tennessee. It was an ancient cave many miles deep that held the bones of Indians who had been hunted down by Andrew Jackson in the early 1800s and of Confederate soldiers who had tried to hide there during the Civil War. Many people had gone into the cave to explore it, only to lose their way in the dark labyrinth and die there over the years.

Johnny Cash knew Nickajack Cave. And in October 1967, he decided to enter the cave, walk deep enough into it to lose himself, and die. Cash carried a flashlight with him (did he have second thoughts?) and crawled ever farther into labyrinthine depths until the flashlight went out. He described the experience like this: "The absolute lack of light was appropriate. For that moment I was as far from God as I've ever been. My separation from Him, the deepest and most ravaging of the various kinds of loneliness I'd felt over the years, seemed finally complete."[5]

Then, thinking he was near death, he said, "I felt something very powerful start to happen to me, a sensation of utter peace, clarity, and sobriety.... There in Nickajack Cave I became conscious of a very clear, simple idea: I was not in charge of my destiny. I was going to die at God's time, not mine."[6]

In utter darkness, feeling his way along ledges and openings, Johnny Cash miraculously crawled out on his hands and knees. How far into the cave had he crawled before turning back—one mile, four, perhaps farther?

When he got out, he found his mother and June Carter waiting for him outside the cave. It was the beginning of a life lived with eyes wide open. "I was ready to commit myself to [God] and do whatever it took to get off drugs," he said of that moment, and "I wasn't lying."[7]

The changes that needed to take place in Cash's life were not the work of a day.

He reported, "Eventually—slowly, with relapses and setbacks—I regained my strength and sanity and I rebuilt my connection to God.... I was able to face an audience again, performing straight for the first time in more than a decade.... God had done more than speak to me. He had revealed His will to me through other people, family and friends. The greatest joy of my life was that I no longer felt separated from Him. Now He is my Counselor, my Rock of Ages to stand upon."[8]

Johnny Cash became filled with the love of God. Through willing, conscious submission to Jesus, he faced his temptations. His life wasn't perfect. He still wrestled with relapses for years, but never at the level of his pre–Nickajack Cave experience. And several years before he died in 2003, Cash recorded the following deeply personal signature song accompanied by his guitar. It's called "Why Me, Lord?" and it asks,

> Why me, Lord? What have I ever done to deserve even one
>   of the blessings I've known?
> Why me, Lord? What did I ever do that was worth love from
>   You and the kindness You've shown?[9]

What helped Johnny Cash change and grow was a dependence on God. The Bible describes this dependence as being "filled" and talks about two types of filling, one from alcohol—the Johnny Cash kind before he walked into Nickajack Cave—and the other from God's Spirit. The biblical challenge is this: "Do not get drunk on wine, which leads to debauchery. Instead, *be filled with the Spirit.*"[10]

> Johnny Cash became filled with the love of God. Through willing, conscious submission to Jesus, he faced his temptations.

This isn't a prohibition against having a beer or a glass of wine. This concerns the *abuse* of alcohol. Most of us know what it is to be filled with or controlled by alcohol. Either you've personally drunk too much or you've witnessed someone else getting smashed. There may have been a time when you thought it was cool to get stupid-drunk at a party. Or maybe you drank enough to work up the nerve to sing karaoke.

But Paul says we should be filled with something else: God's Spirit. It's not a tentative suggestion, a mild recommendation, or a polite piece of advice. It's a *command*.

> We become filled with the Spirit by surrendering to Christ and consciously opening our lives to His filling.

Permit me to get grammatical on you for a moment, because there's a point to it. The verb *be filled* in this verse is in the passive voice, which means that you don't fill yourself—you let the Holy Spirit do the filling for you. In fact, there's one Bible translation that puts it almost exactly that way. "Let the Holy Spirit fill you," it says.[11] Yet at the same time, the filling is not totally passive, any more than getting drunk is totally passive. A person gets drunk by drinking. We become filled with the Spirit by surrendering to Christ and consciously opening our lives to His filling.

The term *be filled* is also in the present tense, which indicates not some dramatic or decisive experience that will settle the issue for good, but a continuous action of being filled. Now, Paul wrote in Ephesians that we have been "sealed" with the Holy Spirit.[12] The term implies that God has marked us as His own with finality. *Boom!*—permanently His. But although all believers are "sealed," not all believers remain "filled," for the sealing is past and finished while the filling is (or should be) present and continuous.

Do you see that?

Once and for all. But also ongoing.

I have a friend named Jon who, when he would see me at church, would hold his hand up in the air with his palm open. I thought it was a little weird.

One day he held up his hand and said, "Jud, do you know why I always do this when you see me?"

"No."

"Because I'm reminding you that whatever battles you are fighting in your life, the answer is to surrender them to God."

> Self-submission, not self-assertion, is the hallmark of the Spirit-filled Christian. We live with open hands of surrender rather than clenched fists of control.

So later that day, my wife, Lori, was frustrated by something. I said, "Lori…" and I opened my palm and raised my hand. Not the best move!

You don't want to try the hand thing in your marriage or with your kids, but the attitude it represents is a good way to live before God. Self-submission, not self-assertion, is the hallmark of the Spirit-filled Christian. We allow ourselves to be filled by taking time to listen to God's Word, communicate with Him in prayer, and meditate about who He is and what He's done for us. We live with open hands of surrender rather than clenched fists of control.

Being filled with the Spirit is a daily, ongoing process by which we allow God to change us for our own good. We experience the excitement of a life that is under God's control. Each day has unexpected challenges and victories, but in the process we are becoming our real selves, filled with God and seeing Him in the details of life.

As Johnny Cash said when he was older and grayer, his craggy face deeply lined, "It's an ongoing struggle. I do know, though, that if I commit myself to God every morning and get honest with him and myself I'll make it through the day just beautifully."[13]

Chapter 17

DON'T STAND ALONE

Becoming the real you God envisions is not a solo thing. You can't do it alone. That's why God created you to belong to a tribe where you can become what He desires.

Your tribe is called the church.

As a teenager, I didn't understand why people attended church. My parents were true believers. They went to church every weekend and dragged me along. While they attended the main service, I convinced them that I went to the youth group. In reality I'd slip out the back door and walk the alleys around the church, smoking cigarettes and waiting for the service to end.

I felt like an outsider as I watched people pull into the church parking lot and walk inside the building. Some looked happy and were excited to be there, some looked frustrated, and some looked tired and bored. *What's the point?* I wondered. In a world filled with injustice, corruption, and death, how could God exist anyway? If He was

> God created you to belong to a tribe where you can become what He desires. Your tribe is called the church.

so great, then why was the world so messed up? And what difference could God honestly make in my life?

I'd hear Christians talk about heaven and hell, but from my vantage point at the time, hell didn't seem so bad. If hell was real, then all my friends would end up there anyway, I figured. And if heaven was populated by some of the people who claimed they knew the way, I wasn't sure I wanted to be with them.

So I skipped church each week. Yet something pulled on my heart. I sensed that I was not right with the world, that there was more to life. Finally, one day I walked across the parking lot and into that church. My addiction to drugs had driven me to personal despair. I knew my life was way out of control, and I knew I needed help. I certainly didn't have all the answers, but for the first time I was genuinely open to exploring my questions.

God, through the people of the church, saved my life. They met me where I was and never judged me. They encouraged me and gave me space to seek answers to my questions. The Bible came alive to me as they guided me in how to read it. I've never gotten over how those people helped me and prayed for me when I was broken and confused. That's what the church should do, what it should be. And that's why I've dedicated my life to helping others who are like me. Walking across that parking lot that day is a decision I have never regretted.[1]

From the beginning, God's dream involved community and friendship for each of us to fully realize our potential. Before the creation of time, He thought of us with love. The Bible says, "Long before he laid down earth's foundations, he had us in mind, had settled on us as the focus of his love, to be made whole and holy by his love."[2]

We were created in love, with love, and by love. This may seem too good to be true, but I've come to believe it precisely because it is so good that it must be true. God spoke creation into being so that we could join His fellowship.

When God was unfolding His creation, He said, "Let us make man in our image."[3] Who exactly is "us" here? No one had been created yet, but God was in community with Himself. The Bible shows God in a community of love, peace, and fulfillment even before the first human came into being.

I admit this is challenging to grasp. Part of God's very essence is community—three persons in one God, the Trinity. Community helps describe God. If He's that way in His very being, it stands to reason that community is an essential quality for the world He has created.

And if we are to live with eyes wide open, if our lives are to be meaningful, it follows that community is vital and fundamental for our life on earth. It's no surprise that in the middle of His creative work, God went straight down the community route.

Seven times in the creation account of Genesis we read how God looked out at His creation and noted that it was good. Yet when He created Adam, He said it *wasn't* good that he was alone. Even though Adam was in a relationship with God, this wasn't enough.

For a time after I became a Christian, I thought that all I needed was God. Yet according to God Himself, I was wrong. I need more than God. I need others, just as Adam did.

God created the first woman as a "helper" for Adam.[4] Behind the Hebrew noun *helper* is the verb *to save*. Eve was created as a savior, Adam's rescuer from solitude.

The Bible is the story of God's dream for community coming to fruition. He started with Adam and Eve and later called together a people, Israel, and united them as His own to enjoy each other and His fellowship. They were to shine the light of His love and goodness to the world. Then Jesus came and began a new community through His death, resurrection, and ascension to heaven. The community of the church was born, a fellowship of diverse people with a common God and goal.

Paul described the all-encompassing, radical counterculture of the church of God—the called-out ones who place their faith in Jesus—like this: "There is neither Jew nor Greek, slave nor free, male nor female, for you are all one in Christ Jesus."[5] In the church there is no place for prejudice between rich and poor, black and white, educated and uneducated, clean and dirty, male and female, even Cowboys and Steelers fans—we are all united in Christ!

The church is a place where the social stigmas that divide us in our culture fade. It's a place where hope and healing are experienced, where grace flows freely and new life is found. This is God's idea, a tribe called out to serve Christ and impact the world.

> In the church there is no place for prejudice between rich and poor, black and white, educated and uneducated, clean and dirty, male and female, even Cowboys and Steelers fans—we are all united in Christ!

I've been around long enough to hear all the excuses for why people don't get into community, why they don't come to church, why they don't get into a small group of other believers. Sometimes people will say to me something like, "I experience God in nature. That's really the way I do it. The mountains are my church. When I'm fishing, that's my worship."

Can you experience God in nature? Absolutely! God created nature. It's a wonderful thing. But can you fully experience what God desired for your life outside of community with other people? No.

I used to work with the homeless a lot as a volunteer. On many occasions I would wake up a guy on the street in the morning. The guy would have several layers of clothes on him. He would smell really bad because he hadn't had a shower in months. He'd be covered with dirt and grime. He had drunk himself to sleep the night before and thrown up all over himself just before passing out. The vomit would be dried on his jacket.

This guy would be at his absolute lowest, the dregs of human society.

Now, having spent several years working with homeless in America, I've learned that this guy may have a PhD, or he may have even been a pastor at one point. You would be amazed at the kinds of people who turn up homeless for various reasons.

When you drop down and look into the eyes of a person at his lowest, you see that he is still more valuable to God than all the

> Although you can experience God in nature, it will never replace the experience of God in serving and helping others or in being an active part of a faith community.

mountains or lakes in the world. Why? Because he's made in the image of God. All those other places were made by God and reflect His magnificence, but they weren't made *in His image*. And although you can experience God in nature, it will never replace the experience of God in serving and helping others or in being an active part of a faith community.

There are times when I'm worn out. I get to the end of the week and don't have my message ready for the weekend. It's Saturday, and we're gearing up for the Saturday-night services. I get a call that somebody is hurting, or maybe someone has lost a child. That stuff weighs heavily on me. So I'm in the car on my way to church, and what I really want to do is drive south on the freeway from Las Vegas to California and the Pacific coast.

But I come to the church and start to interact with people. Some of them may be hurting, and we pray together. Others need encouragement. Some of them will encourage me. I find that the cloud that hung over me starts to lift. I get inspired. Then I come into the auditorium and hear the music. That allows me to get my focus off myself and onto God—onto who He is, onto the bigger stuff of life. I am renewed and encouraged by others.

All this goes to show that I need community. All of us need community. That is how God has wired us. This process of becoming who God desires us to be happens in the context of relationships with others. With others, we drop our masks, share our secrets, and confess our sins. With others on the journey, we experience change, growth, and transformation. It doesn't happen in isolation; it takes a tribe.

Part 4

———

WIDE OPEN
TO INFLUENCE

Chapter 18

Unhindered to Make a Difference

Seeing and living with eyes wide open means we not only embrace God's view of us, along with our new identity, and begin the journey of personal change, but we are also are freed to make our own unique mark for good on our culture.

A while back I was driving down Las Vegas Boulevard, a.k.a. the Strip, near the famous Welcome to Fabulous Las Vegas sign. There I noticed an obscure marker that says "Town of Paradise." Just that and nothing more.

I did a double take the first time I saw it because it captures the essence of what Las Vegas presumes to be. And all in a single phrase: "Town of Paradise."

This "paradise," nestled within the confines of the Las Vegas Strip, is supposed to be fabulous. It's the place where everything comes up twenty-one. Where the world is your oyster...when you're winning. Where you can be anything and anyone you want to be for—let's see, what time does the plane leave?—oh, for about seventy-two hours.

I later learned that there really is a town called Paradise smack in the center of Las Vegas. It was created in the 1950s so that the big hotels that were there first wouldn't have to pay too many taxes to the city. The township encompasses most of the length of the Strip—just wide enough to take in the huge hotels, the glitter, and the fantasy. It was named after one of the early gangland casinos in Vegas called the Pair o' Dice.

It's a tax dodge, see?

What the town of Paradise doesn't cover is the territory where the neon lights grow dim. Where life is raw. Where the pimps and the prostitutes divvy up the earnings. Back in the shadows, where the needles come out after the spotless limousines have pulled away. Where the dealers and the street lords keep one eye on the action and another on the practice of deception. Where everyday moms and dads carve out a living in the suburbs.

> There are two Las Vegases. There's Paradise, which is a figment of the imagination, a commercial convenience where adults live out their fantasies. And then there's East of Paradise, which is the place that corresponds to day-to-day reality.

Think of it this way: There are two Las Vegases. There's Paradise, which is a figment of the imagination, a commercial convenience where adults live out their fantasies. And then there's East of Paradise, which is the place that corresponds to day-to-day reality.

Paradise is the Vegas of the Bellagio with its glorious fountains and the voices of Andrea Bocelli and Sarah Brightman wishing you good night and thousand-thread-count sheets and three-hundred-dollar dinners. This is also the Vegas of cabanas and the beautiful people, leaning against their silk cushions amid the tinkling of ice cubes in crystal glasses.

Then there's East of Paradise, where the sun is pitiless in its intensity. Where the garbage out behind the 7-Eleven bakes in the heat. Where a suburban dad with plenty of money secretly hides his alcoholism and where a successful doctor covers up his gambling addiction. Where the homeless go into storm tunnels at night beneath the Boulder Highway. Where out behind the cement-mixing plant a family of five sleeps in their twelve-year-old car because they were just expelled from Budget Suites.

East of Paradise can be hellish, or even hilarious, depending on the context.

It's a pregnant young woman walking down the street wearing a T-shirt that says "What Happens in Vegas Doesn't Always Stay in Vegas." Then below the words, the shirt has a big arrow pointing straight down to the baby yet to be born.

East of Paradise is where a wife is working 4:00 p.m. to midnight, and her husband is working midnight to 8:00 a.m., and her mom is taking care of their three-year-old each night. And then one day she finds a purse in her husband's SUV with lipstick a color she has never used.

Here's Bart, a guy who came to Vegas and—get this—on his third day in town hit the jackpot for ten thousand dollars. But now it's six months later, the ten grand is long gone, and Bart is sitting inside a casino playing a slot machine at three o'clock in the morning. And it just continues like this. There is day and there is night and there is day again. And inside the casino time as we know it ceases to exist.

And then there's Jenny, who had a relationship that went south in Tennessee. She came to Vegas to get away from the heartache because she could dance as lightly as a fawn. She landed a role in a stage show and felt good about herself again. But eventually the show changed, the director wanted younger girls, and now Jenny is delivering the mail. Soon she'll be fifty. She's the one in the safari hat who gets in and out of her little mail cart and whose legs are now arthritic.

What struck me as I drove past that sign on Las Vegas Boulevard is the irony that I live just east of the worldly paradise, with all the beauty and glamour and popping of flashbulbs and limos idling at the curb. Yet in our own way we are all outside of paradise. We all experience pain and chaos in our lives. We've all had dreams come crashing down. We all know something is wrong, not just *out there,* but *in here* as well.

The Bible sets up this tension from the get-go.

It begins with Adam and Eve living in paradise until they both ate the forbidden fruit from the Tree of the Knowledge of Good and Evil. In one of the most stunning, horrific moments in the story, they both got tossed out of the garden...to the east.[1]

This was cataclysmic—a moment in time when paradise was lost, the world was made radically different, and humanity's intimate presence with God was broken. God put an angel with a flaming sword at the east gate of the garden to guard the way back in. It was over. No instant challenges to some cosmic NFL replay official. No more walking with God in the garden.

God meant business on this one. And ever since that moment we've been east of paradise—way far on the outside. Wondering. Speculating. Trying to get back.

This is more than a flannel-board Sunday school lesson with a tree and a snake and Adam and Eve barely covered by a fig leaf. Think about the horrendous moment when Adam and Eve were banished from the garden.

Here's *Titanic* going down. Eden is being lost. The world as we know it is being forever changed. The Bible pulls no punches in describing this. And after going only a few chapters further into Genesis, we've traveled from paradise to murder, broken relationships, polygamy, drunkenness, and crazy sexual immorality à la Sodom and Gomorrah.

But the good news—the exceedingly good news—is that while the human race is exiled from paradise in the biblical story, we are not exiled from God. The biblical story isn't over yet, and there are enough lifeboats for you and me. There's still God's grace. Because of it, we still haven't perished. And we are called to bring restoration to our world—not to live in a fantasy world, but to bring real change to the real places where we live, with all their desperate needs.

We've seen God's love for us and looked at how we can experience more of our new identity. This change takes time and happens in community, but it is part of becoming our true selves.

In this part of the book we'll consider another aspect of the adventure God has for us. That adventure moves beyond changing personally to changing the world by shaping the culture—east of paradise. We champion the good, the true, and the beautiful in culture and help to restore the world in which we find ourselves.

When you look to the Bible, you discover that it starts with the story of creation and the Garden of Eden, or paradise. Then it moves to the Fall, where Adam and Eve rebelled and humanity entered a new era east of paradise. The story of the Bible then progresses on, through many ups and downs, to redemption in Jesus, and finally portrays restoration.

If we focus exclusively on individual transformation, as we did in the last part of the book, then we have seen only half the story of what God desires for us. The full story includes the call to create culture and restore it. We're called to live out of our unique identity as believers to serve the common good. This chart developed by Gabe Lyons and the Fermi Project illustrates it well.[2]

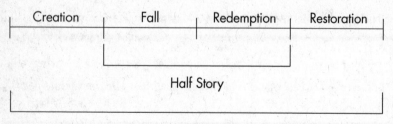

Looking at the chart, you'll notice that the full story of the Bible, and of the real you, involves not only the Fall and redemption but also creation and restoration. After Christ redeems us and forgives us, we are called to use our gifts to influence culture.

Just think about this: when people practice and write law that upholds justice, they engage with God in cultural creation and restore the world. When they join the political process, they serve the common good. When they create amazing works of art, music, and media, they are fulfilling their unique purpose. When health-care professionals go above and beyond to advance medicine or help patients feel comfortable, they serve a greater cause. As scientists explore the dimensions of the universe, they reveal more of God through what He created.

Being the real you involves sharing the unique gifts God has given you with others for the common good.

> If we focus exclusively on individual change and transformation, then we have seen only half the story of what God desires for us. The full story includes the call to create culture and restore it.

The call to influence culture for good, even when our lives are messy, goes back thousands of years. At the end of the book of Acts we read of Paul being under house arrest and chained to a Roman soldier whose duty it was to watch him. Paul couldn't leave. He had just had a tough conversation with leaders in Rome who did not know who he was and who left their meeting debating what he had said. Meanwhile, Christians were being persecuted and suffering for their faith.

Yet despite all of these obstacles, look at how Acts ends: "He [Paul]...was welcoming all who came to him, preaching the kingdom of God and teaching concerning the Lord Jesus Christ with all openness, unhindered."[3]

Unhindered is the last Greek word in the book of Acts. I think it was a deliberate statement by the author. Despite the legal system and the persecution Paul faced, despite the fact that everything seemed hopeless and culture seemed unaffected, Paul was unhindered at the end of Acts because God was alive and working. The term suggests that things were wide open for God to work and for people to be positive agents for change in the Roman culture.

> *Unhindered* is the last Greek word in the book of Acts. I think it was a deliberate statement by the author.

And God did move unhindered through Christians into the culture. Christians brought new life and hope to their world. Rodney Stark wrote,

> To cities filled with the homeless and impoverished, Christianity offered charity as well as hope. To cities filled with newcomers and strangers, Christianity offered an immediate basis for attachments. To cities filled with orphans and widows, Christianity provided a new and expanded sense of family. To cities torn by violent ethnic strife, Christianity offered a new basis for social solidarity. And to cities faced with epidemics, fires, and earthquakes, Christianity offered effective nursing services.[4]

They took their personal redemption and channeled it into cultural restoration. They realized that they were blessed to bless and help others. They had the promise of heavenly paradise, but they also worked hard east of paradise to make a difference. They lived with their eyes wide open. And so can we. We're called not only to see God and ourselves differently but also to interact with the world differently and bring change to our culture.

As you move into the world using your influence for God, you'll feel more alive. You'll sense that you are coming into your own, into the person God created to use for His glory.

Now, in case this talk of cultural restoration strikes you as too abstract, too difficult to apply in your day, let me introduce to you in the next chapter to a friend named Jamie. He'll show you how restoration can start with something as simple as an act of love.

Chapter 19

LOVE IS THE MOVEMENT

It started with a simple effort to help a broken nineteen-year-old girl named Renee. She was caught up in a web of drugs, addiction, abuse, and self-injury. She had already tried to commit suicide a couple of times, and her friends desperately wanted to help her. So they took her to a rehab clinic. But what did the rehab workers do? They sent her away and told her to return in five days.

Five days? For a suicidal drug addict, that's an eternity. What would happen to Renee before the rehab unit was ready to take her in? Her friends would, again, be there for her.

Jamie Tworkowski—one of those friends—wrote of that time, "For the next five days, she is ours to love. We become her hospital and the possibility of healing fills our living room with life. It is unspoken and there are only a few of us, but we will be her church, the body of Christ coming alive to meet her needs, to write love on her arms."[1]

Jamie and his friends ran their own rehab, so to speak, for those five days. They spoiled Renee, took her to rock shows, prayed for her, and helped her stay sober long enough to get into rehab.

Describing the night before Renee finally left for rehab, Jamie wrote,

> She hands me her last razor blade, tells me it is the one she
> used to cut her arm and her last lines of cocaine five nights
> before. She's had it with her ever since, shares that tonight
> will be the hardest night and she shouldn't have it. I hold it
> carefully, thank her and know instantly that this moment,
> this gift, will stay with me. It hits me to wonder if this great
> feeling is what Christ knows when we surrender our broken
> hearts, when we trade death for life.[2]

These words are part of a poetic short story Jamie wrote about their experience titled "To Write Love on Her Arms." To fund Renee's rehab, the group of friends had T-shirts made with the title and asked others to get involved. Soon bands including Jimmy Eat World and Switchfoot were wearing the shirts, and a movement on MySpace to help Renee and others struggling with depression, self-injury, and addiction exploded. It has become a global movement molded around such phrases and initiatives as "Love is the movement," "Rescue is possible," and "Stop the bleeding."

Jamie reflected on what he learned about God and love from all this.

> We often ask God to show up. We pray prayers of rescue.
> Perhaps God would ask us to be that rescue, to be His body,
> to move for things that matter.... It has been simple: Take a

broken girl, treat her like a famous princess, give her the best
seats in the house. Buy her coffee and cigarettes for the coming down, books and bathroom things for the days ahead.
Tell her something true when all she's known are lies. Tell her
God loves her. Tell her about forgiveness, the possibility of
freedom, tell her she was made to dance in white dresses. All
these things are true. We are only asked to love, to offer hope
to the many hopeless.... We were made to be lovers bold in
broken places, pouring ourselves out again and again until
we're called home.[3]

Jamie embodies this in many ways. The first time I met him,
before I knew his story, I sensed compassion and care for people ooz-
ing out of him. He and many like him are shaking things up for
good in our culture. And while the story of Renee's life is still ongoing, she is two years removed from rehab, is remaining sober,
and is living a new life.

What Jamie and others have personified is what the apostle Paul
called the "way of life that is best of all."[4] These words introduce the
famous love chapter of the Bible, 1 Corinthians 13. Love, he was
saying, is the best way to live our lives and relate to the culture.

Thinking along the same lines, John would describe the relationship between how we love others and how we relate to God this
way: "Dear friends, let us continue to love one another, for love
comes from God. Anyone who loves is a child of God and knows
God. But anyone who does not love does not know God, for God is

love."[5] So how we love others has everything to do with our relationship with God.

But here's the age-old question: What *is* love?

Some time ago I watched the Grammys and saw Tina Turner onstage. She's a legend in music and a great performer, and I found myself singing along: "What's love got to do with it, got to do with it? What's love but a secondhand emotion?" It's a classic song, but on this occasion I began to think about the words while I was singing.

> Love is something you do. It's a behavior. You don't just think about it or talk about it—it's active and transformative.

Then I stopped short. Is love just a secondhand emotion? What *is* love?

The Bible says love is a way of acting. Not stage acting, but acting in the sense of thoughtful, premeditated human conduct. Love is something you do. It's a behavior. You don't just think about it or talk about it—it's active and transformative. It's not something you simply feel. Love in its fullest and most developed sense is in the carrying out. It's a commitment to God and your fellow person, a determined way of living. It's helping a young woman stay sober by setting up a home rehab for five days rather than leaving her to self-destruct.

Love motivates us to engage our culture and seek to restore it.

It shows itself in many ways, including in what we say. "If I could speak all the languages of earth and of angels, but didn't love others, I would only be a noisy gong or a clanging cymbal," Paul said.[6] And it is not just that we sound like a noisy gong or a clanging cymbal. That passage literally reads, "I have *become* only a noisy gong or a clanging cymbal." It's as if all those words spoken without love were not only empty but actually changed us for the worse.

For years I heard Christians talk about loving the sinner but hating the sin. Yet when I considered their discourse, what they said and how they said it, I began to feel that they hated the sinner as much as the sin. The reality is that while our harsh words may hurt others, they also *change* us. When we laugh at or make fun of others because of their sex, race, politics, religion, or whatever, it shrivels our soul. It hardens our heart. When we gossip or tell half truths or untruths about others, there's a price to pay. Words have incredible power.

Paul continued by pointing out that all the knowledge in the world is not enough without love. "If I understood all of God's secret plans and possessed all knowledge,…but didn't love others, I would be nothing."[7] All the degrees, all the expertise, all the knowledge amount to nothing without love. Even understanding "all of God's secret plans" amounts to nothing without love.

My friend Kyle became a follower of Jesus, not because he found someone with all the answers, but because he knew someone full of love—his wife, Joy. He wrote:

> For two and a half years she watched as I rejected, investigated, discussed, ignored, and eventually accepted Christianity. Never once did she treat me like a project. Even in my most arrogant and rude moments, when I was pretty much attacking her faith and relationship with God, she seemed almost at peace.

She protected my search when others threatened it. When some "Christians" gave me pamphlets that said convert now or go to hell, she lived out a different kind of message. She lived her life as an authentic Christ follower. She talked about her relationship with Jesus, but she didn't sugarcoat it. She talked about her struggles and her successes. She talked about the things she had answers to but also admitted that she had questions.[8]

Now Kyle is giving back, passing on this love and purpose in his community. He went on to study for ministry in graduate school, and later I had the privilege of being part of his ordination. He now serves students and young people in Portland, Oregon, at a church community.

Love makes the difference. And when you mix faith that God can and will do great things through your life with a genuine care and love for people, amazing things happen.

A couple of years ago, a business leader named Scott Sullivan told me that there were four thousand registered homeless kids in the Las Vegas Valley. They were being fed through the elementary school system on the weekdays, but many of them didn't eat anything on the weekends.

Eventually, Scott started a nonprofit organization called Caring for Kids and began to have strategic conversations with the public school system. We as a church came alongside the organization, and now we are feeding more than seven hundred kids every week. We bag up food for them to take home on Friday after school to get them through the weekend.

One little girl named Sophie said she was so thankful for the food. When asked why, she said, "Because without the food I don't get to eat until school starts on Monday. What I do is take the food bag home, and just before I get there, I go into an abandoned house and hide it. If I take it home, everyone will eat it and I won't get any. So each night I wait until everyone is asleep, and I climb out of the window, go to the abandoned house, and eat."

> When you mix faith that God can and will do great things through your life with a genuine care and love for people, amazing things happen.

This is happening in our cities, in our own backyards. But Scott has shown that we can change the culture through a simple meal.

Today, hundreds of our church members are volunteering, and casinos are busing their employees down to help in preparing the food bags. Together, as casino workers and church people stuff backpacks of food for local elementary school kids, conversations begin to happen—about life, faith, and what it's really about. Perceptions and ultimately lives are impacted. But it goes back to Scott and a group of people who chose to do something about a need in their community. They loved with their actions, not simply their words.

This love can start in the home, as you seek to act lovingly toward those closest to you. Then it moves out to your neighborhood, as you love your neighbor. Maybe that means taking care of the widow's lawn down the street or periodically cleaning her house if she is incapable. Maybe it means taking some time to listen to a neighbor who is hurting. This love spreads into our workplaces. We listen to our co-workers and pay attention to the things they care about. We refuse to engage in gossip about others and seek to encourage and bring hope. Maybe we lead out on a pro bono initiative helping underresourced families at a law firm. Or we go above and beyond in the construction field to do the job right. Maybe we spend some extra time as a teacher with a struggling student to set him or her on the right path. Perhaps we know our own Renee, and we do our best to "write love on her arms."

A simple act of love can shape and restore culture.

Chapter 20

THE CULTURE WAR IS OVER; THANK GOD!

Recently I met Joe Cortez after a weekend service at Central Christian Church. He is one of the great referees in boxing history, having called some of the biggest fights on the planet over the last couple of decades. He's a warm, kind man, and when I met him, I couldn't resist the opportunity to get a picture with him. I called over a friend to snap the shutter, but before he did, Joe held up my hand as if I'd just won the heavyweight championship of the world.

I stood there thinking, *This is the guy who held up Floyd Mayweather Jr.'s hand after he beat the famous Oscar de la Hoya. This is the guy who held up Lennox Lewis's fist after he polished off Evander Holyfield. And this is the guy who refereed the last fight of "Iron" Mike Tyson, once the fiercest, most lethal boxer on the face of the earth.*

I've got the picture framed in my home office, and I love it. I love boxing too. (Please forgive me if you, like most sane people, don't.) Sometimes I use boxing as a metaphor for life. But here's something I've come to realize in recent days: boxing is not the best picture of how the Christian community should engage culture.

For too long we've engaged in culture skirmishes and fights. We've viewed those who believe differently as the enemy, and we've often crossed lines to get a perceived victory. We've been willing to damage a lot of people to have the referee hold our hand up after a bout. The culture war dominated much of the 1980s and 1990s as an argumentative and aggressive political posture, led in many cases by good and well-meaning people. But the posture of confrontation created a widespread perception that Christians believe in their own moral and religious superiority. The posture bullied through certain initiatives but also alienated countless people from the faith.

> I was standing in front of a multibillion-dollar hotel, knowing what Las Vegas is built on, where its roots are, and thinking of the waves of people walking past me. It was like a light came on, and I realized that the culture war is over. And we lost.

A few years ago I had a transformative experience on Las Vegas Boulevard related to this culture war. I was standing in front of a multibillion-dollar hotel, knowing what Las Vegas is built on, where its roots are, and thinking of the waves of people walking past me. It was like a light came on, and I realized that the culture war is over. And we lost.

Let me repeat. *We lost!*

The culture war is over not just in Las Vegas. It's over in New York, Chicago, Boston, Los Angeles, and most other major cities in America.

Sure, my perspective is a little skewed because of living in Sin

City, but the realization that Christians lost the culture war has actually liberated and empowered me. It has forced me to reevaluate how and when I engage culture. Now my calling is to love and accept people one-on-one, caring for them where they are.

My role is subversive as I carry the light and love of Jesus into the streets of my city. I'm trying to flip the perception of superiority and hypocrisy by being honest and straightforward about my faults and my hope for transformation in Jesus. And I'm joining my community in a different culture war—one that attacks poverty, crime, addiction, and pain.

Rather than posture myself as against or above culture, fighting some kind of holy war, I'm finding hope in tomorrow by adopting a couple of important postures.

> I'm trying to flip the perception of superiority and hypocrisy by being honest and straightforward about my faults and my hope for transformation in Jesus. And I'm joining my community in a different culture war—one that attacks poverty, crime, addiction, and pain.

One is a posture of grace over judgment, which can bring great cultural influence. For example, take my friend Sonny. When Sonny first came to our church, he had been living on the street as a crack addict for nine months. He was a mess. But our people didn't judge him; they cared for him. Sonny became a Christian, was baptized, and began a spiritual journey. Eventually people in the church helped him to find a job and gave him a car. He went on to grow and mature and even get married.

Fast-forward four years from the time Sonny walked in off the street. The mayor of Las Vegas tried to pass a law that said you could no longer feed the homeless in any public place in the city. (As background, know that Vegas does not have the social services many other cities have, and it has been voted the meanest city in America to the homeless.)

Sonny was outraged and decided he could not sit by and watch this happen. He legally challenged the law, contending that it was unconstitutional. The first hearing finally came. Picture the courtroom. All the attorneys for the mayor on one side in their power suits. An average guy standing alone on the other side in street clothes. The judge looked over the case and looked to the mayor's attorneys. The judge said that it was unconstitutional to single out one group of people and discriminate against them in this way—and threw the case out!

The reason you can legally give a homeless guy a sandwich on the streets of Vegas today is because one formerly homeless guy named Sonny used his influence.

But would that have happened if he'd first encountered judgment rather than grace in the Christian community?

Influence starts with God's grace, which transforms our lives and culture over time. Rather than protest the moral failure of our community, what would happen if we served them in love? Won't our actions of love and mercy make a greater impact than our picket sign?

I recently had lunch with a friend named Jim Gilmore who wrote an amazing book called *The Experience Economy*. Jim told me, "Authenticity is a big buzzword in the church, but the Bible doesn't use the term. It doesn't talk about authenticity as we do today. The Bible talks about truth. Living in the truth and sharing the truth."

That statement rattled me because I'm always talking about being authentic. Yet I believe Jim was right. The Bible focuses more on truth that makes absolute claims on my life. I should be first concerned about knowing this truth and living in it. By living in the truth, I will be authentic. By sharing the truth of God's Word through my life and love, I will see culture impacted for good. This posture is one of truth over inauthenticity.

> People won't really listen to you until they trust you. When they trust you, you can tell them the truth. Then, even if the truth is hard, they will trust you more, precisely because you told them the truth.

I'm learning that people won't really listen to you until they trust you. When they trust you, you can tell them the truth. Then, even if the truth is hard, they will trust you more, precisely because you told them the truth. Truth must be at the center of our lives and conversations.

It is not truth in a combative sense, truth socked to you by a left hook. It is truth embodied in our lives and lived out in culture. Jim signed his new book *Authenticity* for me this way: "To Jud—Be real. Preach truth." It's an awesome challenge. I pray that by taking a posture of grace, love, and truth we can continue to see cultural change in significant ways.

How is God leading you to create and restore culture? Maybe it is in using music and the arts to bring hope and meaning to our culture. And when I say this, I'm not implying that you need to start a Christian band or do a Christian movie. That may be your calling, but a creative work doesn't have to be specifically Christian in theme to bring glory to God. Arts that focus on the good, the true, and the beautiful can bring restoration to our culture. Maybe you're an architect and you create spaces that seek to restore creation through designs that foster community and increase our ability to relate to one another and accomplish specific tasks. Maybe you're like Sonny and your role in renewing culture is in serving the homeless or launching a nonprofit or encouraging your friends in positions of influence.

As you use your influence, you'll find meaning in helping others and making a difference. You'll discover the real you.

Chapter 21

A FUTURE AND A HOPE

Shakespeare said, "What's past is prologue." He was certainly right when it comes to human events, and he has even proven to be correct when it comes to the newest gizmos and gadgets. Think back ten years. What was your life like in terms of the latest in modern technology?

Ten years ago I had my first cell phone. The battery lasted only forty-five minutes if I was actually talking on the phone. It was the coolest thing going, and I was immediately hooked. I remember that there was a one-line screen on which you typed in the number you were trying to reach. This was *high* high-tech, man. Jud Wilhite, out on the cutting edge.

> The pain, hurt, brokenness, and junk of the past do not condemn us to living the same in the future. We do have hope.

Now, a decade later, everybody has a pocket computer in their phone. My phone plays videos, searches the Web, stores full-color pictures of my family that can be changed and updated whenever I please, features all kind of games...and the list goes on and on.

"What's past is prologue" is true in a spiritual sense as well. Just as we can't anticipate all the social and technological changes we'll face, we can't determine all the personal twists and turns our life and influence will take. But we can look forward with optimism because of the God we serve. The pain, hurt, brokenness, and junk of the past do not condemn us to living the same in the future. We do have hope.

The Bible is a book overflowing with hope. There are well over 150 references to hope in its pages. In fact, Paul called God the "God of hope" and prayed that He will "fill you with all joy and peace as you trust in him, so that you may overflow with hope by the power of the Holy Spirit."[1]

> We usually say, "As long as there is life, there is hope." But I believe that as long as there is hope, there is life.

Psychologist Dr. Harold G. Wolf wrote, "Hope, like faith and a purpose in life, is medicinal. This is not merely a statement of belief but a conclusion proved by meticulously controlled scientific experiments."[2] We usually say, "As long as there is life, there is hope." But I believe that as long as there is hope, there is life.

As I surrender my view of myself and embrace God's view of me, I'm filled with hope. I know that I'm imperfect and that selfishness and sin sometimes get the best of me. Yet God has invested in me, just as He has invested in you. No matter what habits, addictions, or hang-ups we wrestle with, there is always hope to change and become more of who God desires. God wants us not only to experience hope but also to bring hope to others.

Several years ago, in California, I met a teenager named Joshua Sauder who embodied hope. I'd see him navigating his wheelchair around our church campus, talking with friends and sipping a drink. He always had a warm heart, his face was brightened with a smile, and his words were encouraging.

Before he was born in 1984, his mother, Robyn, decided to name her baby Joshua because Joshua was Moses' right-hand man and someone of great strength. It turned out that he would need that kind of power and strength.

The fact that he is alive today at twenty-four testifies to an amazing story of friendship.

He was born on a Wednesday, ten to twelve weeks prematurely, and the following day a tube had to be inserted into his chest to remove an air pocket between his lung and rib cage. On Friday his lung collapsed, and hemorrhaging began in his brain.

Worse was yet to come. Within hours, his vital signs had weakened, his blood pressure was low, his pulse was erratic, his skin was ashen, and his lips were a purplish blue. Joshua somehow survived that weekend.

A CAT scan was performed on Monday, and afterward the pediatric neurologist entered the hospital room where Robyn was sitting and pulled up a chair. "The news I have to share with you is not good," he said. "Your son has suffered a grade-four brain hemorrhage, and the damage is extensive. A grade four is the worst kind. And he now has water on his brain. The long-term prognosis is not good either.

"He will most likely be a vegetable, and you may want to consider placing him in a home. He'll never know anyone or anything. He will never talk, walk, or even think. He will just *be*."

In his first year, Joshua had five operations to remove pressure caused by water on his brain. Today, nearly twenty-five years and more than twenty surgeries later, Joshua is hardly in the vegetative state his doctor had predicted. He lives with cerebral palsy and is not able to use his right arm or either of his legs, but he is very bright.

As Joshua grew up, he excelled in his classes. He also followed sports avidly, reading sports news in newspapers and listening to sports broadcasts. Early in 1994, Josh attended a hockey game played by his favorite team, the Anaheim Mighty Ducks. He also got a chance to meet someone he much admired—Chris Madsen, then the Mighty Ducks' play-by-play announcer. After meeting Chris and receiving his autograph, he began a friendship with the announcer that would have life-and-death implications.

That day, Chris invited Joshua to attend games anytime as his guest. Over the course of the next year, they shared many fun and special experiences "calling" Ducks games together, Chris working one side of the booth and Joshua sitting quietly beside him.

Late that November, however, Joshua became extremely ill. Within a month, he had to have surgery to remove more spinal fluid on his brain. Though he initially recovered well, he was slipping again by the following April. His prognosis was grave. He underwent another brain surgery, and another and another, until five had been performed in the space of a month.

Usually he came out of these operations talking and interacting with others, but after his fifth surgery, he remained unresponsive. Robyn stood by his bed with her pastor, and they did everything in their power to bring him out of his coma, all to no avail. They were close to losing hope, and seemingly nothing could be done.

After several days, Joshua's dad called Chris Madsen and told him what had happened. Shocked, Madsen called Joshua's room. Robyn answered the phone and informed him that she believed Joshua could hear him but simply couldn't respond. She held the receiver down to his ear.

"I decided to talk in a language Joshua could understand and appreciate—sportscasters' lingo," Chris recalls.

"Well, Josh, tonight the Mighty Ducks close out their forty-eight-game schedule against the Toronto Maple Leafs."

Silence. But the call sounded exactly like radio.

"The Ducks, who have lost three straight, will start Mikhail Shtalenkov in goal."

Nothing.

"If the Ducks pull off a victory tonight, they'll finish the season with a record of sixteen wins, twenty-seven losses, and five ties good for thirty-seven points."

Still no reply. Madsen said a little prayer, and immediately it came to him. A familiar battle cry Joshua had responded to so many times before came to Madsen's mind.

He got back on the phone and said, "You know what, Joshua? If I was in that room with you right now, I'd lean way over that bed and I'd put my mouth right up next to your ear, and I'd call out, *Joshua shoots! He scores! Ducks win!*'"

Suddenly Joshua reached over with his hand, brought the receiver up to his mouth, and shouted, "Hello, Chris! How are you?"

Robyn exclaimed, "It's a miracle! It's a miracle. My baby's back. It's a miracle." She sprinted into the hallway, yelling to the nurses, "He's talking! He's shouting! He's talking on the phone!"[3]

There were tears and rejoicing. And since that day fourteen years ago, Joshua has never stopped talking. He later served for four years as manager and public-address announcer for the Santiago High School basketball team in Corona. And in 2003 he walked across the stage with the help of others to receive his high school diploma.

At the end of the 2001–2002 hockey season, Chris Madsen's three-year contract as the voice of the Anaheim Mighty Ducks was not renewed. The job that he had dreamed of for a lifetime and prized beyond all else was gone—and with it, as far as he was concerned, a part of his identity was gone as well. He was now struggling with who *he* was.

Chris returned to California for Joshua's graduation. Driving out to Corona, he wondered if there would be a change in how Joshua would perceive him now that he was no longer the voice of his favorite team.

But as the door to the Sauder house swung open, Joshua came flying across the room in his wheelchair with a grin, extended a high-five with his good hand, and both of them hugged. Then Chris took a tentative step back.

"What?" Joshua asked quizzically.

"I…didn't know how you'd respond," Chris said.

"What do you mean?"

"Well, for one thing, I'm no longer the voice of the Mighty Ducks."

"So?" Joshua shot back.

"So...your broadcasting-booth buddy doesn't see himself as the same person anymore."

"The same what?"

"The same person that I was when I was a TV play-by-play announcer."

With that, Joshua's innocent grin turned into a full scowl. He reached out his left hand, caught Chris by his right forearm, pulled him close, and looked him squarely in the eyes.

"You're not just that!" he said. "You're more than that. And don't you forget it! I care about you for who you are, not for what you do for a living." Suddenly the roles reversed, and Joshua was the one inspiring hope to Chris. And it made a huge difference. In many ways, Joshua saved Chris's life.

Today both of them are influencing culture. Joshua is encouraging people, engaging in broadcasting, and refusing to let his physical challenges stop him. Chris Madsen is now a businessman and sports newscaster in Los Angeles.

We wrap our identity and self-esteem in many things, but God cares more about who we are than what we do for a living. Sometimes—like Chris Madsen—we miss this, and we need others to walk beside us and remind us of our new identity, of the person God created. We need to be reminded that God is not finished with us and that there is hope to change, hope to grow, hope to heal, and hope to reach after dreams and make a mark for Him.

God captured this hope when he spoke to the Israelites through Jeremiah: "'I know the plans I have for you,' says the LORD. 'They are plans for good and not for disaster, to give you a future and a hope.'"[4]

While the context is specific to the Israelites, the promise applies to Christian believers and is consistent with the other promises of God to His children. Think about this amazing promise.

"For I *know*..." Jeremiah wrote.

> God is not finished with us, and there is hope to change, hope to grow, hope to heal, and hope to reach after dreams and make a mark for Him.

God was saying that He is God and knows exactly what is going to happen even before anyone thinks of it or conceives it. Nothing that has happened has ever surprised Him. Nothing that will happen will ever catch Him off guard. He knows exactly what we need, what is coming, and how to empower us to face it. He can help us change, grow, and adapt. He knows how to strengthen us when we're tempted and how to encourage us when we're frustrated. He knows the trials we will face and the losses we'll experience. And He's committed to see us through them.

"...the plans I have *for you*."

God knows the plans he has for the 6.6 billion (and still counting) people on this earth. And that includes you and me! He knows every good and bad moment in our lives and how we will react. He knows the choices we are going to make—the good, the bad, and the ugly. Even now He knows all our future sin and failures…and He still has plans for *us*! He wants to use us to share His love through our actions and deeds. He desires to see us change culture from the inside out.

"They are plans *for good*…"

We've already noted the surprisingly common and thoroughly misguided understanding out there that God is some kind of grinch who sits back and tests you by throwing every imaginable evil circumstance your way. There is evil in the world, yes. The devil is real, and he works against us. But there is safety in Christ, who has overcome darkness with light. God's plans are for good. And as we serve God and help people, we bring that same goodness to others.

"…and not for *disaster*…"

Even in the pain and heartache of life, His plan is not to destroy us but to bring about growth and maturity and ultimately to bring glory to His name. Now, this doesn't mean that very difficult moments won't arise in our lives. God knows that through hard times we learn to rely on Him and often grow the most.

"…to give you a *future*…"

I know how threatening the future may seem. What is it going to be like? Where will we be? What will we be doing? Is there life after the phase we're in? The answer to these questions is that God knows and He is in control. We can't let the future paralyze us; we must embrace it with trust in God.

"…and a *hope*."

Each aspect of this promise builds to hope, and holding on to hope brings renewed strength and energy into life.

God tailors these plans in different ways for different people, but they are always plans for good and always provide a future and a hope.

Circumstances change. But hope overcomes. God has loved us from before the creation of the world. He created us to do good works that He already prepared in advance for us to do. He sees us very differently from the way we're naturally inclined to see ourselves.

No matter how shaky your life may seem, God is still working. He is vested in this process with you. He has plans for you. He has plans for you to see your new identity and live out of that. Plans for you to discover your unique contribution and bring restoration to culture. Plans to live with your eyes wide open and fulfill your unique calling.

Notes

Chapter 1

1. 1 John 4:10.

Chapter 2

1. Luke 15:11–32.
2. According to Jewish oral law at the time, a father could execute his estate—render his will—without being dead. Jewish law stated that the son could sell land from the estate, but those who bought the land could not occupy it until the father had passed away. So the father still had control over some of the son's estate while he was alive. This provision protected the parent from an heir's irresponsibility. In this case, two-thirds of the estate went to the older brother and one-third to the younger who was so impatient for his payoff *now*.
3. Luke 15:17, NIV.
4. Uncensored Grace, www.uncensoredgrace.com/confession/entry.asp?ENTRY_ID=385 (accessed November 21, 2008).
5. Mark 14:36; see also Romans 8:15.
6. See Brennan Manning, *Abba's Child: The Cry of the Heart for Intimate Belonging* (Colorado Springs, CO: NavPress, 1994), 62.

Chapter 3

1. Jud Wilhite with Bill Taaffe, *Uncensored Grace: Stories of*

Hope from the Streets of Vegas (Colorado Springs, CO: Multnomah, 2008), 19–20. Originally published as *Stripped: Uncensored Grace on the Streets of Vegas.*

2. 1 Samuel 13:14.

3. See 2 Samuel 11–12.

4. Psalm 51:3.

5. Psalm 51:4.

6. Psalm 103:12.

7. Psalm 51:13.

Chapter 4

1. Romans 8:31, NIV.

2. See Galatians 6:7, NIV.

3. Romans 8:32, NIV.

4. Romans 8:38–39, NIV.

Chapter 5

1. Romans 8:28, NIV.

2. Gregory A. Boyd and Edward K. Boyd, *Letters from a Skeptic: A Son Wrestles with His Father's Questions About Christianity* (Colorado Springs, CO: Life Journey, 2004), 62.

3. Boyd, *Letters from a Skeptic.*

4. Mark 4:35–41.

5. Mark 4:39. Literally, "be still" can be translated as "be muzzled."

6. Mark 4:40.

Chapter 6

1. Hebrews 13:5.
2. Hebrews 13:6.
3. Genesis 15:1.
4. Hebrews 6:19, NIV.

Chapter 7

1. James 1:23–25.
2. Neil T. Anderson, *Victory over the Darkness: Realizing the Power of Your Identity in Christ* (Ventura, CA: Regal, 1990), 43.

Chapter 8

1. Steve Friess, "Identity Theft in Las Vegas Raises Terror Concerns," *Boston Globe,* March 19 2005, www.boston.com/news/nation/articles/2005/03/19/identity_theft_in_las_vegas_raises_terror_concerns/ (accessed November 22, 2008).
2. 1 Peter 2:9–10.
3. Ephesians 1:3–4.
4. Ephesians 1:4.
5. Richard Severo, "Evel Knievel, 69, Daredevil on a Motorcycle, Dies," *New York Times,* December 1, 2007, www.nytimes.com/2007/12/01/us/01knievel.html?pagewanted=1&_r=1&ref=obituaries (accessed November 22, 2008).
6. Kevin Smith, "Evel Knievel," *the-vu,* August 2000, www.the-vu.com/2000/08/evel-knievel/ (accessed November 22, 2008).

7. Smith, "Evel Knievel."

8. Severo, "Evel Knievel…Dies."

9. Severo, "Evel Knievel…Dies."

10. Smith, "Evel Knievel."

11. Evel Knievel, interviewed by Robert H. Schuller, "Evel Knievel's Leap of Faith," *Hour of Power,* April 22, 2007, transcript, http://hop.crystalcathedral.org/print/display_content .php?id=2404 (accessed November 22, 2008).

Chapter 9

1. Ephesians 2:19, NASB.

2. Romans 6:6.

3. Hudson Taylor, quoted in Watchman Nee, *The Normal Christian Life* (Wheaton, IL: Tyndale, 1977), 57.

4. Romans 6:11.

5. John 15:4, KJV.

6. Romans 6:13, NKJV.

7. Brennan Manning, *The Ragamuffin Gospel* (Sisters, OR: Multnomah, 2005), 30–1.

Chapter 10

1. Exodus 19:6.

2. Revelation 1:6.

3. Eugene H. Peterson, *The Jesus Way: A Conversation on the Ways That Jesus Is the Way* (Grand Rapids, MI: Eerdmans, 2007), 14.

4. Romans 12:1.

5. David H. Stein, *Jewish New Testament Commentary: A Companion Volume to the Jewish New Testament* (Clarksville, MD: Jewish New Testament Publications, 1992), 427.

Chapter 11

1. Leviticus 25:55.
2. Author unknown.
3. 2 Corinthians 12:9.

Chapter 12

1. American Society of Plastic Surgeons, "Plastic Surgery Procedures Maintain Steady Growth in 2007," March 25, 2008, www.plasticsurgery.org/media/press_releases/ Plastic-Surgery-Growth-in-2007.cfm (accessed November 23, 2008).
2. Colossians 3:10.
3. Henry Cloud, "Ingredients of Growth," Cloud-Townsend Solutions for Life, www.cloudtownsend.com/library/ articles/7articles3.php (accessed November 23, 2008).

Chapter 13

1. Matthew 23:25–26, NIV.

Chapter 14

1. See www.postsecret.blogspot.com.
2. Romans 7:24, MSG.
3. Romans 7:24, NIV.

4. John MacArthur Jr., *Romans 1–8* (Chicago: Moody, 1991), 392.

5. Romans 7:25, MSG.

6. James 5:16, NIV.

Chapter 15

1. Tommy Newberry, *The 4:8 Principle: The Secret to a Joy-Filled Life* (Carol Stream, IL: Tyndale, 2007), 11.

2. Newberry, *The 4:8 Principle*, 12.

3. Romans 12:2.

4. Newberry, *The 4:8 Principle*, 9.

5. Philippians 4:8.

6. Romans 8:1, NIV; Jeremiah 29:11; 1 John 4:18; Romans 8:31.

Chapter 16

1. Material primarily taken from Johnny Cash with Patrick Carr, *Cash: The Autobiography* (San Francisco: HarperSanFrancisco, 1997); Mars Hill Church, "The Life of Johnny Cash" video, Sermons from the Pew, December 14, 2007, http://sermonsfromthepew.blogspot.com/2007/12/life-of-johnny-cash.html (accessed November 23, 2008). See also Steve Turner, *The Man Called Cash: The Life, Love, and Faith of an American Legend* (Nashville: Thomas Nelson, 2005).

2. Cash with Carr, *Cash*, 7.

3. "The Life of Johnny Cash" video.

4. Cash with Carr, *Cash,* 230.

5. Cash with Carr, 231.

6. Cash with Carr, 231–2.

7. Cash with Carr, 232.

8. Cash with Carr, 234–5.

9. Kris Kristofferson, "Why Me, Lord?", copyright ©1972, EMI Music. (Recorded by Johnny Cash on *American Recordings,* 1994.)

10. Ephesians 5:18, NIV.

11. Ephesians 5:18, NEB.

12. Ephesians 4:30, NIV: "Do not grieve the Holy Spirit of God, with whom you were sealed for the day of redemption."

13. "The Life of Johnny Cash" video.

Chapter 17

1. Jud Wilhite with Bill Taaffe, *Uncensored Grace: Stories of Hope from the Streets of Vegas* (Colorado Springs, CO: Multnomah, 2008), 169–80.

2. Ephesians 1:4, MSG.

3. Genesis 1:26, NIV.

4. Genesis 2:18.

5. Galatians 3:28, NIV.

Chapter 18

1. Genesis 3:22–24.

2. This chart was on a slide at the Q Conference with Gabe

Lyons, April 10, 2008. Used by permission.

3. Acts 28:30–31, NASB.

4. Rodney Stark, *The Rise in Christianity* (San Francisco: HarperCollins, 1996), quoted in Gabe Lyons, "Influencing Culture: An Opportunity for the Church," Fermi Project,.www.qideas.org/pdfs/shortCulture.pdf (accessed November 29, 2008), 5.

Chapter 19

1. Jamie Tworkowski, "To Write Love on Her Arms," To Write Love on Her Arms, www.twloha.com/page.php?id=6 (accessed November 30, 2008).

2. "To Write Love on Her Arms."

3. "To Write Love on Her Arms."

4. 1 Corinthians 12:31.

5. 1 John 4:7–8.

6. 1 Corinthians 13:1.

7. 1 Corinthians 13:2.

8. From a personal e-mail. Used with permission.

Chapter 21

1. Romans 15:13, NIV.

2. Harold G. Wolf, quoted in Armand Nicholi Jr., "Hope in a Secular Age," in *Finding God at Harvard*, ed. Kelly Kullberg Monroe (Downers Grove, IL: InterVarsity, 2007), 118.

3. Details of this story are taken with permission from Chris

Madsen, *Joshua Shoots! He Scores! The Greatest Call I Ever Made* (Santa Ana, CA: JHF Publications, 2003), 82–3.

4. Jeremiah 29:11.

ACKNOWLEDGMENTS

To Lori, Emma, and Ethan, thanks for all the love, laughs, and support. In the words of one of you, "I love you a jillion zillion million" and am so thankful to be on the journey with you.

A big shout-out to the Central Christian Church family for loving God, for accepting people right where they are, and for allowing me the freedom to be myself. I'm so glad to be part of our community.

To Mike Bodine, thanks for standing with me through the good times and the challenging times and for doing the run together. You are a tremendous leader and friend.

To the Central staff team, including Jon Bodin, Kurt Ervin, Eugena Kelting, Michael Murphy, Geoff Sage, Chris Trethewey, and the others too numerous to mention, thanks for your passionate commitment, for your amazing gifts, and for all the fun! I can't imagine doing what we do with any other team.

Thanks to my friend Bill Taaffe for your terrific gift with words, but even more for your heart for people.

To Chris Ferebee, thanks for your wisdom, insight, and dedication to this project.

To Mike Foster, Anne Jackson, and the Deadly Viper community, thanks so much for your support, challenge, and friendship.

To Ken Petersen, David Kopp, Eric Stanford, and the team of the WaterBrook Multnomah Publishing Group, I appreciate all your work and your faith in the message of this book.

ABOUT THE AUTHORS

Jud Wilhite lives in the Las Vegas area, where he serves as the senior pastor of Central Christian Church. Thousands of people attend services at Central's campuses each weekend, along with a global community that attends online (centralonlinecampus.com). Jud is the author of several books, including *Uncensored Grace: Stories of Hope from the Streets of Las Vegas* with Bill Taaffe and *Deadly Viper Character Assassins* with Mike Foster. Jud and his wife, Lori, have two children and a slobbery bulldog.

Bill Taaffe is a writer and editor whose articles have appeared in the *New York Times,* the *Washington Post,* and *Sports Illustrated,* where he was a columnist and senior editor for nearly ten years. He and his wife, Donna, live in the Las Vegas area with their son.

What happens in Las Vegas...

could change your life.

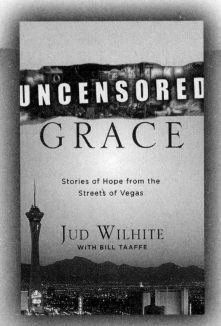

Behind the glitz and glam of Sin City, an amazing story is unfolding. It's a story of what can happen when Christians open their arms wide—really wide—in the name of Christ. *Uncensored Grace* introduces you to card players, exotic dancers, a flying Elvis, an American Idol contestant, and a beat cop turned hero, among others. Each has one thing in common—at their moment of extreme need they encounter an extraordinary God.

Previously published in hardcover as *Stripped: Uncensored Grace on the Streets of Vegas*.